50 Sporting Years . . .
and It's Still Not All Over

Kenneth Wolstenholme

Robson Books

Published in Great Britain in 1999 by Robson Books,
10 Blenheim Court, Brewery Road, London N7 9NT

A member of the Chrysalis Group plc

British Library Cataloguing in Publication Date
A catalogue record for this title is available from the
British Library

ISBN 1 86105 278 2

Printed in Great Britain by Butler & Tanner Ltd.,
Frome and London.

Contents

Preface

I have often been asked why I have never written my auto-
biography and I always said that I didn't think enough people
would want to read it. But at long last I have caved in and
become a slave to the computer, churning out what I hope are
the most interesting facts of what has been a wonderful life for
me. Yes, life has had its ups and downs, but more ups than
downs, I am happy to say. I have travelled extensively to lots of
wonderful places, met many interesting people from all walks
of life, and have to admit that I had the best job in the world.

I had the opportunity to meet and work alongside some of the
great commentators who have graced our radio and television,
including that doyen of commentators, Richard Dimbleby, at a
general election count in Salford, Lancashire. Strangely enough
I lived there at the time and I was fascinated to see how much
Richard had learned about the city in a very short time.

Then there was the great American, Ed Murrow. He told me
how he filmed a long interview just after the war with Field
Marshal Montgomery, whom he admired greatly. During a
break when they were changing the reels of film, Montgomery
told Murrow that he noticed he was still smoking. Ed Murrow
was a confirmed chain smoker and he admitted as much to

Monty, who countered with the question, 'And I suppose like all Americans you take pills for almost everything?'

Ed Murrow agreed he did and added, 'Surely you must have taken the odd pill at some time?'

Montgomery said, 'Rubbish.'

'But surely, sir,' said Murrow, 'you must have taken an aspirin when you had a headache?'

The reply was typical Montgomery. 'Headache, Murrow? Wouldn't tolerate one.'

I mixed mainly with the sporting fraternity. I remember a marvellous lunch with those two firm friends and rivals, Keith Miller and Denis Compton. Keith, incidentally, was a wartime night-fighter pilot and for a time was based at Massingham, in Norfolk. So was I! The food was excellent and the conversation sparkling. Not that I got a word in edgeways, but Keith and Denis never stopped talking, and it was all wit and wisdom. We met at half past twelve and parted at half past six and not one minute was boring.

In Britain we have always been blessed with superb golf commentators, chief of whom was Henry Longhurst, a man of great wit. Once when spending the winter in the Caribbean while we at home were having dreadful weather, Henry ended one of his *Sunday Times* articles: 'I am penning these words on a sandy, sun-kissed beach, with the lovely sea water lapping round my feet. I hope all of you back home are pulling your weight.'

One day a visitor to his windmill home asked Henry how long it took him to write his latest book. Henry put his hands into a tea chest and pulled out a succession of empty half-bottles of champagne. 'Twenty-six half bottles of champagne,' Henry announced. At eleven o'clock each morning Henry would imbibe a half-bottle of his favourite tipple.

Henry's death was a great loss, but Peter Alliss has been a

worthy successor. Peter served his apprenticeship as a professional golfer, unlike most of the present-day tournament players, and this served him in good stead once when commentating on a European Tour tournament. The binding on a club of one of the competitors came apart and the player looked nonplussed. One of his playing partners was Tommy Horton, who, like Peter, had come through the pro's apprenticeship. As Horton repaired his playing partner's club, Peter Alliss gave a running commentary on what to the inexperienced eye looks a most difficult operation. It was a masterpiece of commentary.

Just about every commentary by Peter O'Sullevan was a masterpiece and to listen to him on television was a joy. Peter was such a modest, quiet man that when one of his horses, Be Friendly, won a race on which he was commentating, he still went through the usual procedure. 'And the result is first, Be Friendly, owned by Peter O'Sullevan . . .'

At charity dinners, where part of the entertainment would be the showing of a film of a race of days gone by, Peter would stand up in, say, the Great Room of Grosvenor House, and deliver an off-the-cuff commentary which was impeccable. The man was a genius.

For a few years I did the link job on the golf tournaments, the job which Steve Ryder does so brilliantly these days, but in 1966 the football World Cup meant that I had to step down from the golf. Into my place came Harry Carpenter, and the wretched little man did the job so well that I was out for good. Harry was, and still is, an unassuming man, in the mould of Peter O'Sullevan, but was excellent in his job on golf just as he was as the BBC's boxing commentator. No one will ever forget his rapport with Frank Bruno, whose, 'Know what I mean, 'Arry,' became a boxing catchphrase. Wherever he worked, Harry Carpenter commanded and deserved respect.

The late Brian Johnston was the clown prince of commentators. He never grew out of his fifth-form schoolboy jokes, and brought a lightness of touch to whatever event he was commentating on. Perhaps his finest moment was when he was discussing Ian Botham's dismissal in a Test Match. Botham took a swing at a delivery, lost his balance and although he tried to step over his stumps he failed and his leg knocked off the bails. Johnners, as he loved to be called, said, 'Botham obviously couldn't get his leg over.'

Then followed the hilarious discussion between Brian Johnson and Jonathon Agnew, all round the phrase 'Botham couldn't get his leg over' which reduced the two commentators and the whole listening audience to hysterics.

Mickey Duff is another man I cannot forget. He was a boxing wheeler and dealer, not a commentator. He managed, he promoted and he did just about everything in boxing. The son of a rabbi, he had a few fights in his youth using the name Mickey Duff so that his mother, who hated boxing, would never know he was fighting. Mickey had many friends but also many critics, but in all my dealings with him I always found him straight and trustworthy. He would never go back on his word. Mind you, how he managed to afford to pay his telephone bills is beyond me because he was never off the phone. And he didn't talk into the machine, he *shouted* into it.

There is a wonderful story about the time when he took two of his boxers to Italy. At the airport on the way home they were told the aircraft was full. Mickey blew his top, and he was pretty good at that. He pointed out that he had confirmed tickets, that he was a Jew and that the next day was Yom Kippur, the most sacred day in the Jewish calendar. All the same there was no way he could get on the Alitalia flight and Mickey threatened to sue the airline for every lira it possessed because

Jewish people must be with their families on Yom Kippur.

Suddenly the public address system called for Mickey to go to the Alitalia desk and he was told an aircraft was coming in bound for London and there were seats on it. Mickey calmed down . . . and then boarded the plane for home, an aircraft of United Arab Airlines!

I would never have written this story without giving my sincerest thanks to the directors with whom I had the greatest pleasure of working during my time with the BBC – Alan Chivers, Alec Weeks and the late John McGonagle – three brilliant men to whom I owe a lot and whom I cannot thank enough. I am equally indebted to everyone who worked on the Outside Broadcast Unit covering football. They were all experts at their job and made up a wonderful team, and I am grateful to them all.

Finally, my thanks to Robson Books for publishing my story. I must confess that the manuscript would never have been finished without the encouragement and help I received from my very good friend, Jan Sewell. She not only encouraged me to carry on with the work but painstakingly read every single word, made suggestions, came up with criticism and in short was a tower of strength. There were times when I felt like packing it in, and it was then that Jan poured on the encouragement. So thank you.

And last, but by no means least, thank you all who have bought a copy of my story and I hope you will enjoy reading it.

1

Thank You, Dad

Thank you, Dad should really be the title of this book because it was my dad who first lit the flame of my enthusiasm for football. I was only four years of age when he took me to Burnden Park to see Bolton Wanderers. I have no idea who they played against and cannot remember anything about the game, but what I do remember is that I became a football fan from that very day. And I still am a fan of football and of Bolton Wanderers.

It seems incredible that I saw my first football match just a year after Wembley Stadium was opened. And what an opening it was with first the Empire Exhibition and then that incredible Cup Final in which Bolton Wanderers beat West Ham 2–0. That day 130,000 paid to get into the stadium and my father was one of them. Another 70,000 burst open the doors and got in for nothing, causing tremendous chaos as they poured on to the pitch. An urgent message was sent to a mounted policeman patrolling the West End of London on his white horse. He was ordered to get to Wembley stadium as quickly as he could. He did, and so was instrumental in forcing the spectators off the pitch to allow the game to take place. That is why the very first Wembley final is known as the 'White Horse Final'.

The 1923 final was the start of a wonderful run of cup success for the Wanderers. They reached three finals in seven years and won every one of them. After West Ham, in 1926, they beat Manchester City and then Portsmouth in 1929. In those three successful finals Bolton didn't concede a single goal. That established Dick Pym, the goalkeeper, as my boyhood hero and made me determined to be a goalkeeper. I became one, albeit not of the Dick Pym standard.

Determined to be a goalkeeper I always kept a close watch on other keepers. One I admired immensely (but not as much as I admired my hero, Dick Pym) was Harry Hibbs, of Birmingham. He made everything look so easy. He was never flamboyant but always safe. Then Ted Sagar seemed to play for ever for Everton. He retired after a tremendous career only because, as he told me, the crosses began to come over that bit higher and the low shots came at him that wee bit lower.

Early in my football-watching career I almost brought my visits to Burnden Park to an abrupt end by becoming what can only be termed as football's first hooligan. And I was only about six or seven years old at the time. Derby County were the visitors and for some reason or another I took an instant dislike to them. Maybe they had scored against my beloved team, which I always thought should not be allowed. Whatever they had done I started to scream, 'Dirty Derby', and then began to add certain other expletives which shocked all those around me and especially my father. The strange thing about my outburst was that bad language was never heard at home, so how on earth I had managed to pick up one or two ripe and frowned-upon pieces of the English language I don't know. What I do know is that I was removed from the ground and warned by my father that if I ever behaved like that again it would be the end of my football watching.

But all this is jumping the gun a bit so, let's begin at the beginning. I was born on 17 July 1920 in Worsley, which at the time was a quiet village some three miles from Manchester, but which has grown into what the estate agents call a highly desirable residential area. Even some of the highly paid modern footballers live there these days.

My father, who was called Thomas, was in the cotton trade like most people in Manchester at that time. He was, as you will have gathered, very keen on football and he played for a local Sunday School team called New Jerusalem in Kearsley, near Bolton, where he lived as a young man. He often assured me that he was the finest left back New Jerusalem ever had until a bout of rheumatic fever brought his career to an end, but I have never had any confirmation of that from any other source. One thing I do know is that my dad was so keen on football that he never allowed any member of the family to be married or buried on a Saturday. Saturday was football's day.

My mother showed little inclination towards sport and I don't think many women did in those days. A woman's place then was said to be in the home. But although Mother never took me to football, she often did take me to watch cricket at Old Trafford. Thanks to her I saw some magnificent cricket and some magnificent cricketers. Thanks to her I was able to enjoy as a child such never-to-be-forgotten stars as Ernest Tyldesley, Jack Hobbs, Herbert Sutcliffe, Hedley Verity, Frank Woolley, K. S. Duleepsinghi and many others. That was an education you just couldn't buy. Centuries before lunch were not uncommon in those days, so thanks, Mum, for making it possible for me to see such great performers, even if you did doze off quite often yourself while I was watching.

My mother's maiden name was Redgrave but it was her first name which always caused some amusement among us children. She was christened Euphemia, often abbreviated to Effie. The girls in the family suffered with those names: one who was born and died before I came along was christened Effie, and my eldest sister was called Edna Redgrave. After Edna came three boys, Leslie, Neil and me, and I thanked my lucky stars that they couldn't think of a second name for me so called me just plain Kenneth. My younger sister was saddled with Margaret Effie and she loathed her second name to the day she died.

As we were such a large family we lived, not surprisingly, in a large house, called The Priory. I don't remember a great deal about it because we left it when I was about seven, but I do recall the shower in the bathroom. The shower itself was at one end of the bath, protected by glass on three sides, and the fascinating thing about it was that water didn't only pour down on you from above but also from the sides. I had never seen a shower like that before and I never saw one like it again until 1955 when I became a member of the Royal Automobile Club in London's Pall Mall. To this day the club is famous for its showers, both in Pall Mall and at the Golf and Country Club at Woodcote Park in Epsom. Once when I was playing golf abroad I was asked by a local member which was my home club. When I told him the RAC in Epsom he replied immediately, 'Oh! I've been there. That's the club with the wonderful showers.'

In 1927 the dreadful recession was gaining momentum, although it didn't mean a thing to me. Perhaps trying to wipe the impending doom from their minds, everyone developed Eclipse Fever. Yes, 1927 was the last year a total eclipse of the sun was visible in the United Kingdom, until, that is, 1999.

I remember how we all crowded into the family car and set off in the early hours of the morning for Southport sands. The world and his wife were there, everyone equipped with special eye protection (although nothing like the sophisticated protection given by the 1999 glasses) and I remember I gaped in amazement as slowly but surely everything went pitch black.

The thrill of the eclipse faded into insignificance as the recession deepened. The cotton trade was particularly badly hit. We left the Priory, and instead of going to a public school like Edna and Leslie, or a famous grammar school like Neil, who was a pupil at Manchester Grammar, I found myself at Cromwell Road Council School in Swinton. And I loved every minute of it.

As far as education goes we were given a sound grounding in the three rs, and the more you think of the three rs – reading, writing and arithmetic (there has got to be a little poetic licence somewhere) – the more you realize that those three subjects were the very foundation of learning.

It was a long walk to and from school and we worked hard. We also played hard, but the main game for the boys at Cromwell Road was rugby . . . Rugby League, not Rugby Union. We had a good school team, far too good for me to be a member because frankly I was never any good at the game, but I loved Rugby League, and still do. We were lucky enough to have the school not more than a drop kick away from Station Road ground, home of the Swinton RL Club, one of the best in the league. Not too far away was the Willows, home of Salford, Swinton's deadly rivals. Whenever the two teams met the ground was packed with spectators, and what rugby they saw.

I remember going to watch a Test Match at the Swinton ground – England against Australia. With a number of my school chums I was allowed to sit inside the small concrete wall at one end of the field, just behind the try line. It was a rough, tough game, full of incident, full of excitement and full of fast, skilful rugby. The only thing it lacked was any scoring. Then, in the very last minute, England launched an attack.

My chums and I were sitting on the grass not far from the corner flag at the end England were attacking. The excitement mounted as the ball moved swiftly from one English player to another, then suddenly the England loose forward – I think his name was Frank Butters and that he played for Swinton – broke clear. He was being chased by at least three Aussies so it was touch and go whether he would make the try line before he was grounded.

Suddenly one of the Australians pounced and made a desperate lunge at Butters, who dived for the line at the very moment the Australian grabbed his ear. We had a close-up view of the Englishman touching down for a try . . . and also a close-up view of his ear being partly torn off his head. It was the winning try, but what a price to pay for it. If I remember correctly, Frank Butters wore a skullcap for the rest of his playing career.

Exciting and memorable though that fantastic victory was, there were just as exciting and memorable moments in the schoolboy Rugby League tussles which were organized by the *Daily Dispatch*, one of the Kemsley newspapers produced in Manchester. The *Daily Dispatch* Shield was our FA Cup. In fact it was run on the same lines as the FA Cup, or should I say the Rugby League Challenge Cup.

Schools from all over the area entered and the big prize was a place in the final, which was always played on a senior Rugby League club ground. Warrington, Widnes, Wigan, Salford, St Helens and Swinton had their share of finals, but it seemed to me that Central Park Wigan was the venue which most closely filled the Wembley role. Every season Cromwell Road were there or thereabouts and we always thought that we were the favourites to win the prized *Daily Dispatch* shield.

Sadly, the *Daily Dispatch* which did such a lot for schools rugby, and for our entertainment, went out of business like so many other provincial papers, soon after the Second World War. The main reason was competition from radio and then television news bulletins, which rapidly increased their efficiency and popularity. After all, you had to go to a newsagent and pay for a newspaper; your radio and television news came right to you in your own home, and it was free.

Particularly badly hit – much to my sorrow – were the Saturday-night sports editions. I remember Saturday train journeys when we would rush out of the train at every stop to buy the 'pinks and greens', as we called the sports editions. They were full of results, match reports and news of the local clubs, but excellent radio programmes and then the BBC's *Grandstand* on television put paid to those splendid newspapers. Today it is only cities such as Manchester, Liverpool, Birmingham, Newcastle, Glasgow and some other smaller towns that are still in the Saturday-night business – which is a great pity.

With the death of so many newspapers came the death of sponsorship for schools sport. But the demise of newspapers was not the only cause of the disappearance of such tournaments as the *Daily Dispatch* Shield. Modern school teachers, unlike their predecessors in the old days, are reluctant to give their free time to running sport in their school. On top of that there is a strong wave of opinion which says that we should not be élitist and not encourage competition in sport at school.

That to me is rubbish. Life is a challenge. Life is a competition. So our youngsters should be brought up to be competitive because if they are not they will be unable to cope with the competitiveness of the great big world outside. Those who are competitive will get to the top. Those who are not will be left as also rans. We are not all equal in ability.

But all that and Cromwell Road Council School had to end when the dreaded scholarship examinations loomed. After them I swapped Cromwell Road for Farnworth Grammar School. The first day there was rather frightening because it was traditional for the new boys to go through an initiation ceremony. This consisted of running between two lines of second-year boys, who were all armed with knotted handkerchiefs with which they used to hit the new boys around the head and shoulders. It was a frightening experience that first year, but good fun the following year when we had the knotted handkerchiefs.

Farnworth was a co-educational school with girls and boys sharing the same classroom and the staff consisting of school-mistresses and schoolmasters. Even today I can remember some of them. Mr Weston, a maths teacher, had blond wavy hair and therefore the nickname of 'Perm'. Josh Friday taught physics and was also a brilliant adviser on examination tactics. He followed the horses religiously and was not only an avid student of form but also a great believer that you could work out how often questions came around in the matriculation examination. He would study the questions used in the previous ten years or so and then give his pupils a list of about eight from which the examination questions would be taken. It is said that year in, year out, Josh Friday forecast at least four of the questions that appeared on the big day.

There was a history master who, if he heard talking when he was writing on the blackboard, could wheel round and throw a piece of chalk in the direction of the noise with uncanny accuracy. It was up to you to duck quickly if you were the guilty party. I suppose today he would be sentenced to life imprisonment!

One person stood out in the grammar school staff – Miss Westwood. I went through my whole life thinking, as everybody else did, that she was called Sally. It wasn't until 1999 I discovered that her real name was Sybil. Sybil Westwood – oh, let's call her Sally as hundreds, if not thousands, of Old Farnworthians have always done – was senior mistress and, most certainly, a formidable character. The younger girls seemed to live in dread of her, but as they got older they realized that Sally Westwood was a lady of incredible intellect, charm and kindness. She demanded obedience, though. I remember once one of the junior girls coming into the classroom wearing her blazer. Miss Westwood asked why she was wearing it, to which the girl replied, 'I am cold, Miss Westwood.'

'But it is not cold, is it, my dear?' asked Miss Westwood.

'No, Miss Westwood,' was the almost whispered answer.

Miss Westwood smiled and said, 'So, if it is not cold, you do not need to wear your blazer, do you?' A sheepish 'No' followed and Miss Westwood ended the conversation with a gentle, 'So, take it off, my dear.'

The young girl removed her blazer. That was the power of Sally Westwood.

As well as being senior mistress she also taught her favourite subject, Latin. In her youth she had studied under either Mr North or Mr Hillard, the two gentlemen who wrote what can only be described as the definitive series of books on the Latin language. And Sally Westwood knew them all off by heart.

She was a teacher of infinite patience and skill and it was claimed that none of her pupils had ever failed a Latin examination. She was wise enough not to risk her magnificent record by allowing me to take Latin in my matriculation examination because she knew full well that not even bribery and corruption would have got me anything other than a dismal failure. I think she knew all along that I believed implicitly in the poem:

> Latin is an ancient language, as dead as dead can be.
> It killed the ancient Romans and now it's killing me.

Once when we were studying *De Bello Galico* Book 5 she called on me to stand up in class and translate the first paragraph. I did it perfectly but for one reason only. I sat at the back of the classroom next to the wall on the right-hand side and teachers always picked on that person to do the first translation or answer the first question. So the night before I had found out to my delight that the translation of the first paragraph was in the notes almost word for word.

As I prepared to sit down after what I thought would be acclaimed as an Oscar-winning performance, Miss Westwood handed me the verbal Oscar of, 'Excellent, Wolstenholme. Congratulation, you were word perfect.' Then she snatched the Oscar away by adding, 'Mind you, that is not surprising as the first paragraph is translated in the notes, as you no doubt found out. So would you now please translate the second paragraph.' There were no flies on Sally Westwood!

I left Farnworth Grammar School determined to become not just a journalist but a sports journalist, though, sadly, events beyond my control delayed that ambition for some years. I had many happy memories of my time at Farnworth and was very proud after the war to be invited back to present the prizes at Speech Day.

I know another Old Boy of the school who has never been invited to present the prizes at Speech Day, despite the fact he is one of our most famous sportsmen. His name is Alan Ball.

Yes, *the* Alan Ball who played so magnificently in the 1966 World Cup Final. Bally and I joined forces when it was announced that the school was to be consigned to history and that splendid building was to be pulled down so that flats could be built on the site.

Alan and I lost our battle with the authorities, but that is not all that was lost in the demolition and the last rites of a famous school. The only real landmark in Farnworth was the clock on top of the school. It has never been found since the demolition. Where it is I know not. I haven't got it and I don't think Bally has. But there is a rumour, and it is only a rumour, that a former pupil was so disgusted that the school was being reduced to rubble that he or she nicked the clock and emigrated to the United States.

Not a bad story, is it? Perhaps one day someone will turn the story of the missing clock into a book.

2

The Day War Broke Out

I left Farnworth Grammar School in 1938 with what I called passable qualifications. I had survived the matriculation examination even though I was a good lap or two behind one of my fellow pupils who took nine subjects and gained nine distinctions. I suppose in modern A Levels language that is the equivalent of nine Grade As. That sort of standard was a little (maybe a lot!) beyond me.

However, some people reckoned I deserved an Oscar for a magnificent piece of acting. It all happened on 18 February 1935 at Burnden Park. Bolton Wanderers, then a Second Division side (as, indeed, were Manchester United) were drawn at home in the fifth round of the FA Cup. Their opponents were Manchester City from the First Division. In those days City were *the* team in Manchester with United their impoverished neighbours, so it was no surprise that a big crowd turned up to see the game. After all, the mighty City were the holders of the FA Cup.

Thank goodness our school match that Saturday was a home fixture, and after it a number of us, including my brother Neil, rushed to Burnden Park. We were pretty well the first spectators inside the ground and took up our positions standing right at the front behind the goal at the Great Lever end.

As kick-off time approached people were being allowed to walk round the track which surrounded the playing pitch – in the old days Burnden Park had been the venue of athletic and cycling meetings – and it soon became apparent to us that so many people had got in front of us that we were unlikely to see very much of the game. Cue, then, for the Oscar-winning act. I suddenly clutched the wooden railings in front of us and mumbled that I was going to faint.

Football fans in those days were wonderful people. Anyone in distress was gently passed over the heads of the standing spectators so that they could get help. So as I began to go under there were loud cries for the ambulance crew, those splendid men, women and children – yes, children, too – of the St John Ambulance Brigade, all of whom gave their services free of charge. They were on the spot in no time at all and I was carefully lifted over the railings into the welcoming arms of one of these volunteers. My brother Neil was quick to react and when he said that I was his young brother, he, too, was lifted over the barrier. The other lads got the message and said they were my friends, so they got the caring treatment as well, and as soon as the last one came over the top we all sprinted for our lives. We would have left Linford Christie (or should is be Jesse Owens?) for dead.

We all watched the game lying in the grass just outside the touchline on the Burnden stand-side of the ground. We were level with the centre line so we had a smashing view. In fact, we could have touched the players if we had tried. I wish we had tried because then we might have been able to prevent City romping into the sixth round as 3–0 winners. Mind you, promotion meant more to us Wanderers fans than the Cup in those days. Honest! And we got promotion, taking second place from West Ham United on goal average.

Incidentally, the crowd at Burnden Park that day was a record for the ground of 69,912. And if you are wondering how they squeezed 69,912 people into Burnden Park I can only suggest it was with difficulty.

But let's get back to 1938 when the young Wolstenholme left Farnworth Grammar School determined to be a sports journalist. Off I went for a quick course in shorthand and typewriting at Pitman's College in Manchester.

I spent hours pounding away on one of those glorious old sit-up-and-beg machines, my hands hidden under the shield which prevented me from seeing the keyboard. This was touch typing I was learning and to familiarize myself with the keyboard without ever looking at it, I had to knock out those old favourites such as 'Now is the time for all good men to come to the aid of the party' or 'The quick brown fox jumped over the lazy dog.' . . . or words to that effect. At long last I got the hang of it and went out into the big, bad world to seeking a job. I got one on a weekly newspaper called the *Manchester City News*.

It was there and then that I started to learn about union problems. The *City News* would take on youngsters and teach us the business. Mind you, they didn't pay us anything but they assured us we would learn. Today they call that sort of thing 'work experience'. The National Union of Journalists didn't like it and would not allow any of us to join unless we worked for a newspaper that paid the union rate of wages. But then none of those newspapers would employ any journalist who was not a member of the NUJ. It was the famous Catch 22: you couldn't get a job unless you were a member of the union, and you couldn't join unless you had a paid job. Budding theatricals came up against the same barriers with their union, Equity.

An innocent abroad, I didn't understand such things so I went around pounding the old beat of the parish church, the

Mothers' Union, the police courts and everything and anyone who could produce some news. Weddings were, of course, big stories and you had to get the names of all the guests. 'People like to see their names in the papers,' we were told. Another chore was writing a 'reader's letter' under some *nom de plume* so that the paper could start a campaign which was near and dear to its heart . . . to sell papers.

All those worries about unions, lack of payment and the like began to mean very little in 1938. Europe was on the brink of war because of Adolf Hitler's ambitions, which were described in a joke of the time as, 'Hitler wants peace . . . a piece of this and a piece of that and a piece of the other.' Corny that joke might have been, but anything that made people smile in those days, let alone laugh, was acceptable.

The whole of Britain, indeed perhaps the whole world, was relieved when the Prime Minister, Neville Chamberlain, got off the plane at Croydon and waved that piece of paper in triumph. It contained a solemn pledge from Hitler that he would stop his aggression. There was going to be no war. Sadly, Hitler's solemn pledges were worth just about as much as a football contract is worth nowadays.

Gradually everyone came to terms with the fact that war was becoming more inevitable with every passing day – everyone, that is, except the *Daily Express*, which boasted Britain's largest circulation at the time. The *Express* promised us every morning that 'There will be no war this year, next year or in the foreseeable future.' Every morning more and more people came to believe that the *Daily Express* was being far too optimistic.

Being just eighteen years of age at the time I realized that if war came I would be one of the first to be called into the services. To make sure that I had some choice in the matter I decided to join one of the forces' reserve units.

I thought first about the Royal Navy but realized I had never done any sailing except for rowing a boat once on Heaton Park lake near Manchester. So I didn't think I was cut out for a life on the ocean waves. And what about the Army? Well, if I had to go to war I didn't fancy walking there. All of which left the Royal Air Force. Now that was something else.

Flying was all the rage at the time, although it was a complete mystery to the vast majority of the population. The personalities to whom we all looked up were not the film stars or other entertainers but the intrepid pilots who flew all over the world in flimsy-looking aircraft and set up record after record. People such as Jim Mollinson, Amy Johnson, Amelia Earhart, Jean Batten and Charles Kingsford-Smith. They were the idols of the younger generation.

So the Royal Air Force it was. Off I went to Manchester, had a medical and signed on. I was accepted as a trainee pilot and went to Barton airport just outside Eccles, which is near enough to Manchester, to start my training.

We had to turn up every other weekend and stay for the complete Saturday and Sunday. There was nothing spartan about it: we had a lovely restaurant, excellent lecture theatres and comfortable lounges, and on top of that we were paid ten shillings and sixpence a day – at the time a most generous remuneration. And why so generous? Well, as pilots-to-be we had to hold the rank of sergeant pilot because no one under the rank of sergeant could be a pilot in the RAF. And ten shillings and sixpence was the daily pay of a sergeant.

Most of our time was taken up being lectured about such subjects as Theory of Flight, Air Navigation, Engines and things like that, and if you got more than one half-hour spell of instruction in the air per day you were very lucky.

The very first trip as a mere 'sprog' – RAF slang for beginner – came under the heading of 'air experience'. We were taught how to strap ourselves into the rear cockpit of a Tiger Moth and then an instructor would taxi across the grass (there were no concrete runways at Barton) and take off. It was a bit startling at first seeing the ground disappearing below you. You must remember that very few people had flown before the war so we had no previous experience of being in an aeroplane.

It was a gentle little ride lasting about a quarter of an hour with the instructor talking to you over the simple intercom system and putting you at ease. He explained the basic movements: if you push the joystick forward the nose of the aircraft will dip, pull the stick back and the opposite will happen. Similarly with the wings: push the stick to your left and the left (port) wing will go down, push the stick to the right and the right (starboard) wing will drop. Your feet were on the rudder bar, which caused the nose of the aircraft to move left or right. So, to make a turn to the left, or to port as we had to call it, you needed to move the joystick to the left and apply a little left rudder and, hey presto, you were turning left.

If you sounded quite confident the instructor would ask you if you would like him to loop the loop, the simplest and perhaps the best known act in the aerobatics' book. Suddenly the nose of the aircraft would drop and you would be hurtling towards the ground. Then the joystick would be eased back until you were in a vertical climb. As the nose of the aircraft started to fall away at the top of the loop you imagined you were in grave danger of falling out. But there was no such danger. Centrifugal force pressed you harder than ever into your seat. It was a comforting thought, just as the safe landing was a comforting experience.

That was the first hurdle safely cleared, but in the future it was a case of doing it all yourself, albeit under the watchful eye of the instructor, who always sat in the front cockpit and could take over the controls whenever he thought it necessary. The hardest part about flying is not so much about what happens in the air, but rather getting the aircraft up into the air, and then down again. In other words, circuits and landings, or as they were disrespectfully called, circuits and bumps. The landing is the hardest part of all because you have to gauge how far you are off the ground and when to bring the throttle right back to execute what is called a three-point landing. With the bigger aircraft it is easier because you can almost fly them right into the ground, whereas with a lightweight Tiger Moth you had to stall and land gently.

That is why a Tiger Moth was such a wonderful aircraft on which to learn to fly. It had such gentle habits. If you tried to land at too high a speed, the Tiger Moth would bounce, so you had to be spot on every time. You also had to fly with the very minimum of instruments to help you, so learning on that wonderful De Havilland aircraft was not easy. But it was rewarding, and I have never heard anyone who learned on Tiger Moths, or who has flown them later on in his or her life, say one single word against them. On the contrary the Tiger Moth has been rightly called the best aeroplane ever built and I once read that someone had said that the day they closed the cockpit on flying machines was the day they ruined flying as a pleasure.

One very important thing we had to learn was what causes a spin and how to get out of one. With a Tiger Moth it was difficult to find out. You could throttle right back so that you had little or no power and pull the nose so that your airspeed would fall away to stalling speed, which was very low in a Tiger. Then you had to kick on the rudder bar to get the aircraft into a reluctant spin. And you had to keep the pressure on the rudder bar to keep the aircraft in the spin before you made your recovery. Rumour has it that there was an instructor at Barton who would put a Tiger Moth into a spin and then raise his hands in the air to show the pupil he wasn't holding any controls. 'Don't worry, my lad,' he would tell his startled pupil, 'these things get out of a spin on their own and in their own time.'

Ah, they don't make aeroplanes like that any more.

Many people think that the greatest moment in your flying career is the day you get your flying badge, or wings as they are called. It isn't. The greatest day, the most momentous day, the day you will never forget, is the day you go solo for the very first time.

You never know when the moment is coming. You will land the aircraft after yet another lesson and taxi in. The instructor will tell you to stay where you are for a moment and then he will climb out of the cockpit on to the wing and carefully make his harness safe. He will jump down to the ground, stand alongside the rear cockpit and utter those never-to-be-forgotten words, 'Well you're on your own now. Just take off, do a circuit and land. Good luck.'

With that he walks away, leaving you with a smile and a wave, not to mention a mouth that is as dry as a desert, a heart that is beating at a rate that would cause a panic in an intensive care unit, and two legs that are rivalling your hands in the battle of the shakes. Everything you have been taught has gone into a muddle. You try to remember. Put the nose into the wind, open the throttle slowly, when you've got enough speed help to lift the tail, when you come unstuck (leave the ground) climb slowly to about 800 feet then turn slowly to port, at 1,000 feet you should be downwind. You wonder if you've done anything wrong but then you realize you are on the final approach. Watch your airspeed, don't let it get too low, don't let it get too high, lose height slowly, don't keep pushing the nose down and then pulling it up again. Then the final plea of, 'Please God, get it down safely.'

Believe me, you taxi in and climb out of the aircraft feeling the happiest man on earth, and you don't even worry when the instructor walks towards you and says, 'Not the best landing you've ever done, but always remember it's a good enough landing as long as you can walk away from it. Well done.'

As 1938 turned into 1939 the clouds over Europe became ever blacker, until on 1 September Hitler, who had told Mr Chamberlain that he had no more territorial demands, invaded Poland. That evening the wireless (as the radio was then called) announced that all reservists of any of the armed forces should report immediately to their town headquarters. It sank in that the order meant me.

I went upstairs to pack a bag, but how was anyone to know what to pack? We of the RAF Volunteer Reserve hadn't got any uniform so what were we expected to wear? How much should we pack when we didn't know where we were going and for how long we would be there? As I pondered on these problems I could not help thinking about that piece of paper Hitler had given Mr Chamberlain. Whatever happened to it? I still wonder today where it is. What a historic document, a document of deceit.

Once I had packed it was a case of saying, 'Goodbye, see you soon' just as thousands of other young lads were doing. My mother had lost her young brother in the First World War, the one that was meant to end all wars, and she naturally burst into a flood of tears. As I left to catch the bus into Manchester she was still crying.

It didn't take me long to get to the Manchester headquarters, where I was met by a state of 100 per cent chaos, or as the RAF always put it 'SNAFU' (situation normal all f— up). We had all obeyed the orders relayed over the wireless and turned up, to be met by an AC2 (aircraftman second class, the lowest form of life in the RAF) and a sergeant, as far as I can remember. They were both so bewildered they almost enacted a Robb Wilton comedy act on the lines of 'The Day the War Broke Out'.

Eventually the sergeant decided he would have to show some authority so he ordered the AC2 to 'get them fell in'. We poor souls hadn't the faintest idea what he was talking about, but the airman managed to get us 'fell in' in three lines. He went through what we were soon to regard as the equivalent of cockpit drill, giving us orders in rapid succession of 'Attention. Stand at ease. Stand easy,' then back to 'Attention.' He then handed over to the sergeant, who went through the same rigmarole. With us all standing to attention he came out with another Robb Wilton line of 'We are awaiting our orders so could you come back tomorrow.'

I got home just in time to grab some fish and chips which someone had brought in from the local chippy, and just in time to comfort my mother, who had burst into tears the moment her youngest son walked through the door.

Back to Manchester on the Saturday for the same bit of nonsense and an order to 'Come back tomorrow'. This time we stood to attention as the Prime Minister spoke those chilling words, 'So a state of war now exists between the United Kingdom and Germany.'

State of war or no state of war we were asked to . . . yes, you've guessed it . . . come back tomorrow. Then it was come back every other day until it was decided that we should stay at home until we were needed. And when we were needed it was not to go flying but to undergo something they called 'initial training'.

3

Testing the Water

The call to initial training was a few weeks in coming, but eventually it arrived and I was sent to Trinity Hall, one of the famous colleges of Cambridge University. At long last I was kitted out with a uniform and then went through the horrifying experience of mass inoculation. There was quite a crowd of us sergeant pilots and a host of doctors, although I was certain one or two of them were local butchers. Anti-typhoid and anti-tetanus jabs were compulsory and were given, believe it or not, in our chest.

Now needles I hate, always have done and always will do. Even today, when the injections are much more civilized than they were in the old days, doctors and dentists have to ask me politely to relax instead of being so tense with fear that I'm making their job more difficult. But the experience at Cambridge is something that has stuck in my memory all these years, not, funnily enough, because of my fear of the needle but because of what came afterwards . . . the after-effects and someone called Warrant Officer Tynan.

Warrant Officer Tynan soon became more than someone. He was the station warrant officer and quickly turned into one of the most hated men at Trinity Hall. We learned early on that all ranks in the RAF (officers and other ranks, as they are called) fear the Station Warrant Officer more than they fear the Chief of the Air Staff. Warrant Officer Tynan's first action after the gang-bang inoculation session was to look in disgust at all of us who just wanted to sit down and rest and announce that we would all go on a route march for a few miles. With a wicked smile on his face he told us that the exercise would help the stuff which had been pumped into us to circulate through our bodies and ease any after-effects. No wonder he earned the nickname of Warrant Officer Tyrant.

Perhaps the trouble was that few if any of us had met a real disciplinarian before, and Warrant Officer Tynan was a strict disciplinarian. He believed that orders were made to be obeyed, that smartness was essential, and woe betide anyone who disagreed with him. He knew full well that we were all new to square bashing and that we thought that since we wanted to be pilots it wasn't necessary for us to be able to march and excel at drill. He was right. That was exactly what we did think. When an aeroplane flew overhead he rubbed salt into our wounds by bringing us to a halt, roaring 'Eyes upwards' and then proceeding to tell us that we were looking at the real RAF and maybe some time in the future we would be a part of it.

Frankly, most of us would have loved to throttle him, but I am glad that not one of us tried to do it because once we had left Trinity Hall and become part of 'the real RAF' we all realized that far from being a tyrant he was a gem. He knew that in the services, especially in time of war, discipline is essential. We would all have to work as a team and there would be no time for questioning orders, no time for slackness.

The man we all, in our ignorance, hated turned out to be a great man. He took charge of young boys and turned them into young men who, thanks to him, had the grounding which they would later realize was so essential. We never forgot him and he never forgot us. I know that because when I was commissioned as an officer he sent me a note of congratulations. He sent me another when I was awarded my first Distinguished Flying Cross.

I don't know whether he is still alive. If he is I send him my good wishes. If he isn't I reckon he will be taking the parades up in heaven, seeing to it that the pearly gates are well polished every day. Or else!

Having had my fill of marching, slow marching, wheeling, right turning, left turning and about turning I was posted to Sywell, in Northampton, for some more elementary flying training on Tiger Moths. I didn't stay there long because I had almost come to the end of elementary flying before the war started, but Sywell will always have a place in my heart because it played such a part in my future life.

I still looked forward to fulfilling my ambition of becoming a sports journalist, although such peacetime activities seemed light years away at that time. Then one day I started to talk to the timekeeper, the chap who logged our times of take-off and return. It seemed to me an awfully boring job, but he told me that he had suffered from tuberculosis and was therefore not in demand by any of the services though in need of an outdoor job for his health's sake. During one of our conversations I asked him what he had been doing before he became ill and he told me he had been a journalist. The man's name was Harold Mayes. Happily he made a complete recovery, went back to his old profession and I met him again later in my life with very happy results.

After finishing elementary training everyone was classified either as a prospective fighter pilot or a prospective bomber pilot. I have no idea how the selection was made but I do know that I went into the bomber stream which meant that my advanced training would be done on multi-engined aircraft, which in those days meant twin-engined planes. I was posted to Shawbury in Shropshire and had to learn to fly Airspeed Oxfords, which I remember to this day as having the gliding angle of a brick. Mind you, it could have been worse. I could have been trained on Avro Ansons.

Not that I had anything against Ansons. How could any Mancunian say a word against an aeroplane made by that splendid Manchester firm of A. V. Roe, the firm which was to make the Lancaster bomber? The trouble was that the Avro Anson didn't have a hydraulic undercarriage system, so the wheels had to be wound up immediately after take-off and wound down on the landing approach. Each operation took something like 100 laborious turns and it is easy to guess who did the turning. Yes, the pupil, not the instructor.

As a matter of fact I did fly Ansons on one of my rest periods from an operational squadron. It was at Millom, where the airfield was right on the coast, very close to Barrow-in-Furness. (Incidentally, RAF station Millom now houses one of Her Majesty's prisons.) My job was to fly the aircraft which was navigated by pupils who had just arrived from their training in Canada. This meant that I wasn't short of undercarriage winders, but it also had its drawbacks. Having been trained in Canada, the pupil navigators had no idea of wartime conditions. Many of them wanted to smoke in the air, and all of them were bemused by the lack of lights on the ground, which meant that their dead reckoning had to be spot on because to the north of the airfield was the menacing Black Coombe mountain while to the south was the equally menacing balloon barrage protecting the Barrow shipyards. We had some scary, scary nights!

Shawbury was a pleasant so-called permanent station. That meant that it wasn't a collection of Nissen huts but a good peacetime station. But like Millom it had its worries. The Welsh hills were not far away and the dreaded Wrekin kept everyone on their navigational toes just as Black Coombe did at Millom.

Sadly, one or two people did succumb to the Welsh mountains and/or the Wrekin, but after a not very long concentrated course of flying and navigation we were all ready for the next step up the ladder. And this was a big step. Hitherto we had been taught the basics of flying and of navigation, because in those days the pilots were expected to be as competent at navigation as the air navigators. Once we left Shawbury we were to face another problem at our operational training unit.

The OTU was the last posting before the move into the big time, to a fully operational squadron. As pilots we had to learn to fly the operational aircraft. My OTU was at Upwood, not far from Peterborough, and the aircraft we flew were Bristol Blenheims. It wasn't all that difficult for a pilot to get to know the Blenheim, but it was something new to be taught to be the captain of the aircraft and to be the leader of the crew. It would not be unusual for the pilot and captain to be non-commissioned and the navigator, say, to be a flying officer, but, irrespective of rank, the pilot was always regarded as the captain of the aircraft. On the ground the flying officer was the senior who had to be obeyed, in the air it was just the opposite, the non-commissioned pilot was the senior.

There were two types of Blenheim in service with the RAF. The short-nosed Mark One had been replaced by the long-nose Mark IV, which we flew. It was regarded as the latest thing in bomber aircraft and the air recognition handbooks which were sold to the public gave it the highest praise possible. It was alleged to have a top speed of over 300 miles per hour, and I can only say that it might have reached that speed with full throttle in a steep dive.

There were just three to the crew of a Blenheim, the pilot, the navigator and the air gunner, who had a cold, uncomfortable, lonely and highly dangerous position in a turret midway between the cockpit and the tail. The Blenheim was an all-metal construction and it was a desperately cold aircraft to fly in.

At OTU we practised all those skills we would expect to use on operations. We did a lot of formation flying because it was essential in daylight operations for the formations to be very tight. We even did formation flying by night. We often practised low flying, much to the annoyance, no doubt, of the local residents.

All the time the powers-that-be were trying to sort out the crews, and once they had made their decisions the men they had chosen flew together. I had as an air gunner a little cockney lad called Tales. He was a sergeant, as was I. Our navigator came from New Zealand, from Hataitai, near Wellington. His name was Colin Wilson. In March 1941, the three of us said goodbyes to our Operational Training Unit at Upwood and headed for 107 Squadron of No. 2 Group. Their base was Wattisham in Norfolk but at the time of our joining the squadron was on attachment at Swanton Morley in Norfolk.

Now the game really was going to start.

4

Sister Laurence Mary

No sooner had we checked in with 107 Squadron than we were on the move. We decamped locked, stock and barrel on attachment to Leuchars in Fife. RAF station Leuchars, separated only by a strip of water from the home of golf, St Andrews. We were moved primarily in order to attack targets in Norway and just off the Norwegian coast and to keep a kindly eye on the merchant vessels which had to ply their trade in what could be the most hazardous waters of the North Sea.

We were warned from the start that visibility was often poor to very poor in those parts with sea mists, fog and just about everything else you can think of. We were told that if the merchant vessels or their naval escorts saw an aeroplane appearing from out of the gloom, they would not hold a committee meeting to decide whether it was friend or foe. They would open fire at once and if they did any damage to what turned out be a friend then they would be sorry but . . . No one could blame them for that, but I must admit that it was scary flying low over the sea in dreadful visibility and suddenly realize that you were going to fly right over a ship. If it was an enemy ship it would open fire. If it was a friendly ship it would do exactly the same thing. So it was a very quick turn either to port or starboard.

I blotted my copybook very early on in our stay at Leuchars. In bad visibility I landed at the nearby station of Crail. I came in too fast and too high and it became very obvious that it was odds on that I would run out of runway and perhaps go over the cliff edge, which would not be very pleasant. So at the last minute I decided to do a sharp turn to the left off the runway. A bit of left pressure on the rudder bar and we seemed to be doing all right until the pressure became too much for the undercarriage, which collapsed.

The three of us got out safely enough, although I do remember that Polly, as we called Colin Wilson, got a slight cut on his hand. The emergency services were on the spot in no time at all, and only a whisker behind was the station commander. He wanted to know who was responsible 'for all this', and as I began to explain what had happened and why, and what I was trying to do when the accident happened, the station commander leaned against the aircraft and rested his right hand on the pitot head.

The pitot head was the means by which the airspeed indicator in the cockpit worked and was situated under the aircraft's nose. In very cold weather – and it was a very cold day – we kept the pitot head heater switched on to prevent any icing which would lead to the loss of the airspeed indicator. That day the pitot head heater had been on for just over three hours and was still on because I thought the sensible thing was to get out of the crashed aircraft without giving a moment's thought to things like pitot head heaters.

You can, then, imagine what happened when the station commander got hold of the red-hot pitot head. He let out a howl which was surely heard for miles and was hurried away for medical treatment. He never did learn what had caused the accident or what I had been trying to do, and I have a feeling that he didn't give a damn. All I know it that we never met again (thank the Lord) and I have never received a Christmas card from RAF Leuchars.

During our stay at Leuchars we sometimes moved up to start an operational flight at Wick, a remarkable town in the north of Scotland which tried to cater for all tastes by having a building which was a cinema some evenings and a dance hall on others. For the cinema-lovers that was fine but for the dancers it was not so fine. The floor was raked at an angle from the front row of the stalls so that nobody had difficulty seeing the screen, if that is what they had gone to the cinema to do, but on dancing nights it was difficult to do a smoochie waltz when you were dancing uphill.

Apart from my own crew I also became friendly with Alf Groves, who was the air gunner in the flight commander's crew. Alf came from Mobberley, a lovely village in Cheshire, not all that far from Manchester. Before the war he earned a living as an assistant golf professional and his last job had been giving private lessons at a club in, of all places, Hamburg. He was attached to the Wilmslow golf club in Cheshire, but went to Hamburg for a month to coach the son of a German who had been a guest at Wilmslow.

Being a professional he was allowed to go on to the hallowed turf at the Old Course at St Andrews and one day he asked me to have a go at hitting the ball. Now I had never held a golf club in my life so I made an awful hash of it. Alf just looked at me and commented, 'You swung that club like a bloody great tart that's never had it.'

It was about fourteen years before I ever swung a golf club again.

Sadly Alf didn't survive the war.

The squadron spent just over two months at Leuchars before moving back south to Great Massingham, a satellite station to West Raynham in Norfolk. The people there went out of their way to make us feel at home.

One of the villagers' great ideas was to challenge 107 Squadron to a cricket match on the village pitch. This challenge was accepted and I am sure we batted first. I cannot remember whether we won the toss and batted or whether the villagers put us in as a friendly gesture. What I do remember is that one of our middle order batsmen hit an ultra quick half-century before retiring. When later the same player came on to bowl, he proceeded to terrify the locals with his long run and his very, very quick deliveries.

He turned out to be Man of the Match without any doubt and it seems the local vicar told the squadron commander, 'If the good Lord spares that young officer he should develop into a fine cricketer.' Then and only then did the squadron commander reveal the identity of the 'young officer'. He was W. J. Edrich, yes, the famous Bill Edrich, whose splendid performances with bat and ball for England, not to mention his great partnerships with Denis Compton for Middlesex, had already made him a sporting idol.

Bill was an amazing character. He was married five times and never lost his eye for the ladies. After the war he continued with his successful career in cricket and he was always present at the St George's Day luncheon in London. If was after one of these long and liquid get-togethers that Bill died. At his funeral someone remarked, 'I've never seen so many of Bill's friends in one place before. Well, not with everyone sober.'

It was a pity 107 didn't stay longer at Massingham because

later in the war another famous cricket all-rounder was stationed there. It was that great Australian, Keith Miller, a man and a cricketer highly respected throughout the world. He loved his horse racing as much as he loved his cricket and he always enjoyed touring England because there was so much racing and he seemed to be able to find enough time to go and watch it.

Keith Miller was a fearsome cricketer, a tremendous hitter of the ball and a deadly opening bowler. But he was a player you could trust. Sir Frank Worrall, one of that great West Indian 'W trio' of Worrall, Weekes and Walcott, told me a story about him which typifies the man.

The West Indies were batting on an easy wicket in a Test Match in their homeland. They had scored well into the 500s for the loss of only a couple of wickets and the spectators were bored out of their minds. Some, in fact, preferred to sleep in the sunshine.

When Australia recalled Miller for another spell of bowling, he approached Worrall and said, 'Look, Frank, the spectators are bored stiff so let's waken them up. In this coming over the first, third and fifth deliveries will be spot on a length and no trouble to you. But the second, fourth and sixth will be vicious bouncers just over your head.'

Worrall paid Miller the greatest compliment by agreeing to the plan because he knew that the Australian would keep his word. After the first bounder the spectators started to murmur. After the second they began to show their anger. After the third they were in the mood to tear Keith Miller to bits. And at the end of the over, Miller walked towards Worrall and said, 'Well, that's woken the buggers up, Frank, so let's start enjoying the game.'

I remember Keith Miller telephoning me at home and suggesting we met for lunch in the Cricketers' Club. Keith had long since retired and he said he would also ask Denis Compton along. We arranged to meet at half past twelve and I arrived five minutes late, by which time Keith was halfway through his first pint.

Compo, as Denis was called, arrived at half past one, which was punctual for him, so we settled down for lunch and the talking began. Well it began for Miller and Compton. They had a duet while I just sat and listened. It was fascinating and I only wish I had recorded the whole conversation. Suffice to say that I just managed to catch the 19.10 train home out of Waterloo station.

I have rather strayed from the goings on at Massingham . . . One day I shall never forget is 21 May 1941, when the squadron made its second daylight low-level attack in eight days on the fortress of Heligoland. We were briefed to fly in formation at a height of 50 feet and it was hoped that we would surprise the defending forces. We were told to beware of the flak ships and if we were spotted by them to abort the operation. The flak ships served two purposes. They were small craft well equipped with anti-aircraft guns and they were also in radio communication with the mainland. So if they spotted any enemy aircraft approaching they could start firing and also warn the defences on the mainland that an attack was imminent.

We took off just after two o'clock in the afternoon and the weather was not in our favour. It was too nice, the visibility so good that the odds of our creating a surprise were nil. As we neared Heligoland we could see the flak ships dotted around the island. They began firing and the aircraft to my right suddenly turned left and began to climb. I push our nose down to avoid a collision and then it was a mad dash towards the steep cliffs of the island. For a horrible moment I thought I was going to fly straight into them but at the last moment I pulled the control column back and just managed to make it.

Suddenly there was a loud explosion as our aircraft suffered a direct hit. The cockpit filled with smoke and by the time it cleared a little we were on the other side of the island. We had obviously been badly hit, and then I noticed that Polly was injured. Another look told me he was dead.

I remember turning to port to go round the north of the island, but as I dived towards our height of 50 feet above the sea I noticed I was heading straight for another flak ship. All the Blenheim had in front was a fixed Browning .303 so more in hope than anger I gave a burst, hopefully straight at the flak ship. As I headed away from the island I saw two Blenheims to my left so I edged over and tried to join them. Once I had succeeded, one of the Blenheims hit the sea.

I later found out that the aircraft that went down into the water was piloted by Bob Ratcliffe. He and his crew got out into the dinghy, where sadly the navigator, Doug Craig, died. Bob and his air gunner, Jack Smith, were picked up by the Germans and taken prisoner.

That they were picked up was due to the bravery of Flight Sergeant Roy Ralston, the pilot of the other Blenheim. He climbed to 1,500 feet and sent out a wireless message in plain language, knowing that the Germans would intercept it and be able to get a fix on the dinghy. Not until he was certain the Germans had been given sufficient time to get their fix did Roy Ralston stop circling the dinghy and set off for home. By doing what he did, Roy Ralston risked his own life because by that time the skies were alive with German fighters. But it was an act typical of Roy Ralston, who was a brilliant pilot and along with his navigator, Syd Clayton, formed just about the best and certainly the most popular crew on the squadron.

With Roy Ralston circling the ditched Blenheim I was left on my own. It was a long way from Heligoland to Massingham and the aircraft had suffered a number of other hits apart from the main one. With German fighters around the safest thing to do seemed to be to stick close to the sea and hope that nobody spotted me. When we got fairly close to friendly land, we sent out a signal so that the controllers could get a fix on us. That would be a help in case we had to ditch in the sea.

Happily that didn't happen and we were ordered to land at West Raynham, a permanent pre-war station that had far better emergency services than Massingham, to which it was a satellite. What a feeling of relief we had when the undercarriage touched the runway and the aircraft came to a halt.

You might think that the trip to Heligoland would leave me with bad memories of Massingham, but any bad memories have been wiped away by an amazing lady called Sister Laurence Mary, a Daughter of Jesus, of Massingham St Mary. She and four other Sisters live in a convent retreat which during the war years was the Officers' Mess.

The people of Massingham have never forgotten the war and the crews who flew from there. They have formed a History Society which will take over from Sister Mary, who has done all the hard graft of recording everything that happened when the village was an important air base. It was she who compiled the Roll of Honour for those who lost their lives while stationed in the village, collected photographs and kept in touch with so many survivors of the Massingham days. That in itself must have been a monumental task because 'her boys' as she likes to call them are scattered to the four corners of the earth.

The graves of all those who lost their lives while serving at Massingham are in the churchyard, kept immaculate under the supervision of Sister Laurence Mary. She makes sure there are always flowers – posies, as she calls them – on each grave, and on Remembrance Day each grave has a poppy on it. Polly Wilson's grave is there and I must say it brought a lump to my throat when I visited, to discover that it was so well kept and that a young man from New Zealand was still thought of by the Sisters and the locals of a little Norfolk village.

It was a proud day for Sister Laurence Mary when, on Saturday 26 September 1998, the Roll of Honour she had compiled with such care and devotion was dedicated at a special service in the parish church of St Andrew, Little Massingham. And nothing pleases her more than when an old boy of Massingham, or a relative of someone who served there, visits the village. The airfield is no more, but thanks to a devoted Sister nobody has been forgotten.

5

Bomber Command

It is ancient history now that we did not make a very auspicious start to the war and all the aces seemed to be in the hands of the Germans. The RAF was equipped with aircraft largely approaching their sell-by date. The good old faithful Hurricane was doing a marvellous job in Fighter Command and the faster Spitfires were coming off the assembly lines in ever increasing numbers.

Bomber Command was not all that well off. Single-engined Fairey Battles had done all they could in the early months, but it was obvious that the Blenheim would be unable to handle all the jobs it would be expected to. As far as the heavies were concerned, the Hampdens and the Whitleys were old fellows awaiting retirement. They were too slow, too cumbersome and didn't carry the sort of bomb load that was needed. The Wellington did a magnificent job, but it was obvious that if we were going to turn from the defensive to the offensive then the aircraft industry would have to come up with something out of the ordinary.

It did just that, and did it so well that one cannot help wondering what on earth happened to the industry when peace came. We produced the Comet, which had all sorts of troubles from which other manufacturers could learn. The Vickers Viscount was a sensation when it came into service with what was then British European Airways, and Concorde was the wonderful result of Anglo-French industrial skills. But then our aircraft industry slowly but surely faded from sight.

Some of the industrial scrapping did not take place on a level playing field. The rest of the world insisted Concorde had to impose a levy on the first-class fare to prevent British Airways and Air France from attracting the business traffic. This sort of move hardly came within the realm of fair competition, but the Americans were determined to corner the transatlantic market, and corner it they did. It was, though, sad to see the British aircraft industry suffer after the superlative work it achieved during the war under the most difficult of conditions.

The industry knew that we needed big, heavy bombers which could carry huge bomb loads and have, at the same time, the speed and the manoeuvrability which were needed to launch a full-scale attack on the enemy. The first product, the Avro Manchester, was a failure because it was under-powered, but as Avro went back to the drawing board, the industry produced the Halifax and the Stirling. Both were a vast improvement on what the RAF had, but even they were reduced almost into insignificance by the arrival of the king of the heavy bombers from the A. V. Roe stable . . . the Lancaster.

Here was a great aircraft, powered by four Rolls-Royce Merlin engines, which enabled it to carry a larger bomb load than any other aircraft in service on our side, or on the other. In addition, the Lancaster was able to carry the huge blockbuster bombs which were being manufactured. The Lancaster became the flagship of the RAF's heavy bombing campaign and there wasn't another heavy bomber anywhere in the world to touch it. The Flying Fortress, of the United States Air Force, carried a puny load compared with that of the Lancaster, which had a crew only slightly more than half the crew of a Fortress.

The Lancaster was so versatile. It could carry a heavy load of bombs to far distant targets and it could carry out precision bombing at low level with extreme accuracy – witness the dambuster raid led by Guy Gibson.

To many people the Lancaster seemed the ultimate, and who can blame them? But from the De Havilland stable came an aircraft which defied description – the Mosquito. Like the Lancaster it was powered by Merlin engines, but it had only two of them. It was an aircraft designed to do everything and anything, but no matter what it was called upon to do the Mosquito carried a crew of just two – a pilot and a navigator. It was designed to carry no guns whatsoever. The idea was that its super streamlining and its powerful engines would give it a speed which made it a match for almost any fighter.

A story went round the RAF – whether it is true I know not and I doubt whether we will ever find out. According to legend, some characters from the Air Ministry could not agree to the design and felt the aircraft should have a rear turret. So De Havilland built one, and on the test flight it was obvious that the Mosquito had been stripped of all its advantages.

Anyway, the Mosquito was sent into action without a single gun with which to defend itself. It was designed as a bomber which could operate at low level and at over 30,000 feet. So successful was the aircraft that it was also used for photographic duties and there was a version with fixed guns in the nose. This one was used as a night fighter and as a low level fighter-bomber.

I first became acquainted with the Mosquito when I was posted to No.1655 Conversion Unit at Marham in November 1942, and two months later joined 105 Squadron at the same station. Perhaps the first time the Mosquito really hit the headlines was on 4 February 1943 when Squadron Leader Ralston led the first daylight air strike on Berlin, with, of course, a Mosquito aircraft. For the trip to Berlin the Mosquito could carry a two-ton bomb in the bomb bay and a 500-pound bomb under each wing.

Squadron Leader Ralston was the same man as Flight Sergeant Ralston who was with me on the Blenheim attack on Heligoland. He and his navigator, who was Sergeant Syd Clayton before he was commissioned, made up a brilliant team and fully deserved their quick promotion and their various decorations. Once, I was told, they were in a Mosquito over France when they spotted a troop train approaching a tunnel. As the train disappeared into the tunnel they released a stick of four bombs. The first one sealed the entrance to the tunnel, the second damaged the roof and the third and fourth bombs blocked the exit. It might seem a tall story but it wasn't.

The Mosquito proved itself so versatile that it was difficult to find a job it couldn't do. In fact, a special force was set up, called the Light Night Strike Force (LNSF). It was under the command of Air Vice Marshal Don Bennett, the Air Officer Commanding No. 8 (Pathfinder) Group. The members of the Light Night Strike Force didn't do marking duties but they were used very successfully as decoys and as nuisance raiders.

They would attack a number of targets each night and spray 'window', the device which upset the enemy radar, and would therefore create a diversion from the main attack of the evening. They would, of course, bomb their own targets with great accuracy and at one time they were known as the scourge of Berlin, where they went almost every night (or so it seemed). Berliners were woken by the sirens and had no idea whether their visitors were six or seven hundred Lancasters or a dozen

Mosquitoes. Some people wrote off the LNSF as an irrelevance, but after the war, with the benefit of hindsight, everyone realized what a great job it had done.

There were, in fact, many powerful people who thought we should have concentrated on the production of the versatile and speedy Mosquito because the damage it could inflict was out of all proportion to its size. It was also a tough aircraft which could absorb heavy punishment. This, some people found hard to believe, because it was made entirely of wood and was held together by glue. All the furniture manufacturers in the East End of London were recruited to produce the various parts of the Mosquito and they did a great job. Not only could the Mossie, as the aircraft was affectionately called, take heavy punishment from anti-aircraft fire and from the cannon of opposing fighters (if they could catch it) but it could hold its own in a collision. There was one occasion when a Mosquito landed at night followed by a 'wounded' Halifax, which landed on top of it, and the Mossie's undercarriage didn't even buckle. Yet those who had to crash-land their aircraft were delighted to discover that it had the good manners to disintegrate around them on impact, so reducing the risk of serious injury to members of the crew.

The aircraft was not without its bad habits, though. The two in-line Merlin engines were so close together that if you were not very careful you would find the aircraft swinging violently on take-off. There was a strict rule that you should not attempt to take off on a swing. Most of those who tried to do so paid a heavy price for their error. Furthermore it was not the easiest of aircraft to get out of in a hurry. To jettison the hood and climb out of the top was known as the suicide route. The only safe(?) way was for the navigator to unlock the hatch on which his feet were planted. He then had to turn round and face the rear and leave feet first, taking care that when the wind caught his legs

the back of his head did not make heavy contact with the floor
of the aircraft. And if it was in no way a happy exit for the
navigator, for the pilot it was one long horror story. The aircraft
now had a gaping hole just to his right. He had to feather both
engines and try to trim the plane for a gentle descent. Then he
had to undo his harness and pull the intercommunication leads
off his helmet, or risk being strangled the moment he left the
aircraft and felt the leads becoming tighter and tighter around
his neck.

Then it was a case of getting out of the pilot's seat, carefully
turning to face the rear and standing on the nose side of what
was now a very small escape hole in the floor of the aircraft. His
exit route was now exactly the same as the navigator's – gently
lowering himself through the hole in the floor, hoping not to
bang his head and then being able to grab hold of the ripcord
after the count of about three. Then, by the grace of God, he
could float gently down to earth, hoping not to have to face a
battery of fire from the ground troops who were feeling not best
pleased and only too anxious to give a warm welcome, or that
he didn't float gently into the sea.

All I can say is that I am glad I never had to do it.

There were times when the Mosquito had to play an
unfamiliar role. Our highly sophisticated equipment had a
limited range so if the heavy bombers were going too deep into
Germany we would mark a secondary target or attack certain
strategic airfields on the continent. Like many other aircrew I
didn't see the point of this, but after the war I received a letter
from a member of an RAF association. A former Luftwaffe pilot
had written a piece for their newsletter under the heading 'The
Saga of the Other Side of the Hill'. I cast aside my doubts about
the sense of our airfield bombing after reading this account from
a German pilot from Eppstein, whom I have never met but

whom I would love to meet even after all these years. His name was Emil Nonnenmacher, and this is what he wrote:

The most serious calamity the German night fighters suffered in late 1944 was the permanent threat posed by a little insect called Mosquito. Not the ordinary 'Anopheles Malaria' but an aircraft built of wood. And its bite was worse than causing some sort of illness. It meant death to many night fighters.

Many of you bomber lads may have asked the question, 'What are these Mossies up for anyway, if they couldn't protect us by doing some close escort?' From hindsight I can say that quite a number of your bomber crews owe their lives to these Mossies.

Up to 1944 we had been superior in most respects. Any decision as to how to act in combat was ours. This was when some sports among us had their great time. Half a year later we were to learn how bomber crews must have felt in the past years when being sitting ducks to a night fighter. Now we were to know the other side of the medal.

Of course, you bomber boys would not have recognized the trouble these Mossies caused to a night fighter. But here is just one example.

It was the Nuremberg night at the end of March 1944. Twenty of our aircraft were to scramble shortly before midnight. The bombers were approaching abeam Brussels. (We were not stationed ahead of the bombers to lay a trap as is claimed in some dubious books!) Four of our aircraft were already off. I was number five when a Mosquito dropped some bombs in front of my just rolling aircraft. [Actually the load dropped was one target indicator for following aircraft and three 500-pound high

43

explosive bombs – K.W.] Postwar information told me that the Mosquito involved was ML938 piloted by Flight Lieutenant Wolstenholme with navigator Flying Officer Piper.

I managed to cut the power and bring my aircraft to a halt. The bombs had perfectly hit the junction of two crossing runways. Everybody seemed to have been confused and all aircraft were held on the ground until further notice. After a while I took a chance to get off via some taxiways. It was just after midnight but I caught up with the bombers in the Nuremberg area and managed to shoot down a Lancaster.

All the rest of our group were delayed for up to an hour and they totally missed the bombers. Only the first five of our aircraft managed to see any action and together we shot down eight aircraft. I would not hesitate to say that the conditions to bring down a bomber were so excellent as never before or thereafter. Thus this one Mosquito prevented some of the heavy bombers from becoming an equally easy prey. If the other fifteen aircraft of our group hadn't been held up from reaching the scene that night in time to make contact they would have added quite a few more to the total score. (The RAF announced the loss of ninety-seven aircraft on that raid out of a total of 800 starters).

If we had known about the Nuremberg story before the end of the war we would all have been convinced that the airfield attacks were worthwhile.

It is only fair to say here that I have immense admiration for the courage and airmanship of Herr Nonnenmacher. To have bombs exploding in front of you as you start to take off is bad enough, but then to take off on the taxi track not knowing how many more bombs were on their way is simply magnificent. He must have been some pilot, and I trust that Herr Goering suitably rewarded him.

105 Squadron was a happy squadron. There was an excellent rapport between the aircrews and the ground crews. After all it was the ground boys who kept the aircraft in 100 per cent working order, so we had a lot to thank them for. To maintain the close friendship between us it was an unwritten squadron law that at least once a week the aircrews and the ground crews would get together in a local pub, and about once a month the commissioned officers would be invited to a party in the sergeants' mess. Don't run away with the idea that life was one big party, though. Yes, we knew how to let our hair down, but there was a lot of flying to do. When it wasn't operational flying it was training, such as perfecting our techniques with the latest equipment.

Before every operation each aircraft on the battle order had to be tested by its crew. This entailed taking the aircraft up and testing everything – the sophisticated electrical equipment, the performance of the aircraft, the lot. Both engines would have to be feathered (shut down) but one at a time, please. There were cases when pilots pressed the button to feather the port engine to see how the aircraft behaved on one engine. Then, in error, instead of pushing the controls which would restart the port engine, the button to feather the starboard engine was pressed. That left an aircraft with both engines not working, which caused not a little panic until both engines were restarted. Understandably, no pilot would ever admit to having dropped such a clanger.

As the aircraft taxied in after the air test the crew would be waiting for the report from both the pilot and the navigator. Nobody listened to the report more keenly than the flight sergeant, the boss man of the ground crew. Slackness and carelessness he would not tolerate.

His name was Flight Sergeant Sergeant, or Chiefy Sergeant as everyone called him, using the RAF slang term for a flight sergeant. He knew full well that the pilots could not stand any marks on the windscreen. Even the tiniest spot put us off. You might think that was nothing to worry about, but in the air over enemy territory a tiny spot could be a not very friendly night fighter. So the windscreens had to be spotless.

If they weren't, or if there was any real complaint about the aircraft after an air test, woe betide the ground crew because our flight sergeant was a perfectionist. Chiefy Sergeant had a routine which put the fear of God into every member of the ground crew. He would grab his forage cap with his right hand. That was the signal for the ground crew to 'get on your marks'. If he took off his forage cap, that was the signal of impending trouble, so it was equivalent to 'get set'. If he flung his cap on the ground that was the ultimate danger signal for the ground crew to 'go, go, go' as fast as their legs could carry them. If he stamped on his cap, even the aircrew would disappear.

He thought the world of both the aircrews and the ground crews and we all thought the world of him.

For some years after the war I got a Christmas card from him, but he just signed the card 'Chiefy Sergeant' and never gave any hint of his address. Then the Christmas cards stopped coming and I was left wondering whatever happened to Flight Sergeant 'Chiefy' Sergeant. I still wish I knew.

When we had any free time we played a lot of sport at Marham. Mixed hockey was the least favourite sport because the fellows soon discovered that women can do all sorts of evil things with a hockey stick. Clean sports, like football and rugby, were very popular.

One day I was invited to play in a rugby match but I said that if some real rugby player was available I didn't want to rob him of a game. None was available so I agreed to turn out. The lads knew that I was a goalkeeper at soccer so they figured out that I must be able to catch a ball and to kick it. Every time I caught the ball there was a great cry of 'Kick it.' So I did. The snag was that I rarely found touch because I didn't discover until half-time that in those days it was permissible in Rugby Union to kick the ball into touch on the full. The only rugby I had seen or played was Rugby League, where the ball had to bounce before it went into touch otherwise the game would re-start with a scrummage on the spot from which you had kicked.

On another occasion I was asked to referee a game between two sections on the station. It was the final of an inter-section tournament and the excitement and partisanship was much more evident than at a Rangers – Celtic 'Old Firm' game. I was doing pretty well – I thought, anyway – until one side went on the attack. I could see they wanted to get the ball out to the left wing, but I could also see that the player on the left wing was offside. Sure as God made little apples, the ball was swung out to the left wing, and like the good referee I thought I was, I blew the whistle and gave a free kick for offside.

There was pandemonium among the spectators and some foul insults were flung at the poor referee, who was only doing his job like the fair-minded citizen he undoubtedly was. It was a dreadful way to treat an officer and a gentleman.

Well, it was, until the embarrassed referee saw that a defender was standing alongside the goalkeeper and therefore playing the attacker well onside. It was at that moment I decided that I would never referee another match and that all referees must be masochists.

Our sporting days, though, were soon over. On one sad day I broke my left wrist playing in goal and two other aircrew suffered shoulder injuries playing rugby. The powers-that-be then issued an order that in future operational aircrew would not be allowed to take part in dangerous sports.

Just prior to the invasion of France, which heralded the start of what was called the 'Second Front', the squadron moved from Marham to Bourn and shortly after that I got the news that I had been awarded the Distinguished Flying Cross. I wrote a letter home to give them the glad news and my father sent a telegram to my eldest sister, who lived in Cornwall. Unfortunately, in wartime telegrams usually meant bad news, such as that someone was missing or dead, so my sister burst into tears and asked her husband to open the telegram. He did so and said, 'Nothing to worry about. Kenneth is alive and has just been decorated with the DFC.'

All leave for members of the armed forces had been cancelled as soon as it was decided that we would invade France, but operational aircrews were exempt from this. We were still allowed our seven days off every six weeks. I arrived back from leave late one afternoon and found the aircrew lounging around in the mess. It was going to be a 100 per cent effort that night, which meant that every available aircraft and every available crew would be flying.

The following morning I got on my bicycle back into camp – all the aircrew were billeted in Nissen huts outside the camp perimeter in case of air attacks – and the guard saluted smartly and said, 'Well, it's started, sir. We've invaded Norway.'

I nearly died. What comedian, I wondered, decided that we were to invade Norway and stretch our lines of communications so much. It was a relief to find out that it was Normandy we had invaded, not Norway! I sympathized with the guard. After all, when you've been on duty all night it is easy to confuse Normandy with Norway.

The air offensive hotted up after the invasion, with attacks on the flying bomb sites and on targets which would help the Allied armies in their absence. One such attack was made rather dicey for the troops because a couple of Spitfires tried to have a bit of fun. Pip Piper and I were flying in the reserve marker aircraft during an attack on the crossroads at Villers Bocage, and therefore had to orbit the target area in case we were needed to drop more markers for the main force of 270 Lancasters.

We got the order to go in to do precisely that and as we settled down flying straight and level for the aiming point, Pip noticed two fighters above and behind us. He identified them as Spitfires just as our bomb doors were open and we were on the point of dropping the markers. The fighters swooped down to attack and Pip yelled, 'Dive my side.' I did, and the two Spitfires flew past us, waved and waggled their wings in a gesture more friendly than their original one. Nevertheless, they had ruined our approach, which was over the Allied troops and it was impossible for us to renew our run-in. The only thing we could do was to set course for home and jettison our markers into the approved area in the English Channel.

When we tried to do so we discovered we had no markers on board. Pip, who had the release button in his hand when the mock attack was made, must have inadvertently pressed it when he ordered me to dive. So because two Spitfires, finding life boring due to the absence of enemy planes, decided to have fun with a friendly aircraft, the Allied troops had to withstand the shock of target indicators exploding about a thousand feet above their heads. Fortunately all the main force aircraft had unloaded their bombs so no real damage was done. Nevertheless, a heated complaint from the army had reached Bomber Command before we had got back to our base.

With the Second Front well under way the RAF discovered it had a surfeit of pilots, so a lot of us old stagers were given our redundancy notices. We were now available for other jobs in the service.

6

The Gambler Who
Only Lost Five Bob

As I was now no longer required as an operational pilot I was ordered to go for an interview at, of all places, Cranwell. Cranwell was, and still is, the RAF equivalent of the Royal Navy's Dartmouth College and the Army's Sandhurst and when I arrived there I discovered that it was the home of 100 per cent bull. I can't remember how many times I was saluted as I walked towards the Officers' Mess. It all seemed more like a detention camp than a happy station.

Once there I met other redundant pilots who had also been summoned for interview. None of us was ecstatic about things, and it wasn't surprising that after dinner we degenerated into the party spirit. After all, the ante-room, as they called it, in the Mess was about as exciting as watching grass grow. Nobody spoke to anybody so we decided to liven the place up.

We were gentlemanly about it, though. Before we started to sing the more well known of the RAF songs we did give the WAAF officers the warning by singing 'Goodnight ladies'. Some took the hint, others didn't. I suspect they wanted to find out what a real RAF party was like. I won't go into what songs we sang or what games we played but suffice to say we were very raucous and, perhaps, a long way from being officers and gentlemen. The following morning, as we piled into a lecture room feeling very much the worse for wear, we were convinced that something would be said. And it was. A squadron leader told us that he had heard about our behaviour the previous evening and that we should be ashamed of ourselves. He also informed us that a report would be going to our home units. Things looked pretty grim, until he began to tell us why we were there.

He pointed out that if we wanted to stay in aviation after the war the flying instructor's course we were being offered would be of great advantage to us because we would be taught to fly properly, not in the slapdash manner in which we had been flying on operational squadrons.

That was music to our ears. Once Air Vice Marshal Don Bennett, the Air Officer Commanding No. 8 Group, the Pathfinder Force, got to hear that his pilots had been accused of flying in a slapdash manner, he wouldn't give a tuppenny toss about our bad behaviour in the hallowed Cranwell Officers' Mess the evening before. Every single one of us went back to his squadron and told the full story of how we had been accused of being slapdash pilots. Every single squadron commander felt it was an insult to his squadron so the protests went to group headquarters and then to Bomber Command.

We didn't hear a single word about our antics in the Mess.

I didn't want to stay in aviation after the war. I wanted to be a sports journalist. So did another pilot, called Tubby Wills. You could call Tubby Wills the prototype of the Teletubbies. (If you are still alive, Tubby, as I hope you are, please accept my apologies for that.) Like so many of us, Tubby was asked to sign a form saying whether he would be interested in applying for a permanent commission in the RAF come peacetime. He replied, 'I thought I had a permanent commission.'

He had a lovely sense of humour. Once someone told him he drank too much and if he didn't stop he would die young. 'Rubbish,' was his reply. 'I had an uncle who drank a bottle of whisky a day and he lived until he was forty.'

I had heard that there was a public relations department within the RAF so I thought that with my experience in journalism(!) and as an operational pilot I had all the qualifications needed for a job there. Nevertheless, I was surprised when I was called to the Air Ministry for an interview with the deputy director of Public Relations (Service). It was explained to me that there were two deputy directors, one a civilian and therefore a civil servant, the other a serving officer. That was the gentleman I had to see.

He was Air Vice Marshal Lord Willoughby de Broke and before the interview I was told he was a senior steward of the Jockey Club. I walked into his office, saluted smartly and Lord Willoughby got up from his chair, put out his hand for a handshake and greeted me with, 'Ah, yes, Wolstenholme. Glad to meet you. Hang your hat on the rack and take a seat.'

I was more than a bit taken aback and even more so when he offered me a cigarette. Like most people at that time I indulged in what I was to discover was such a bad habit, and we had a short and friendly chat at the end of which he told me he would be delighted to have me in the department. He told me that the PRO who was attached to No. 4 (Bomber) Group was being posted to the Far East and he wondered whether I would be willing to take over at 4 Group's headquarters in York. I was willing, so Lord Willoughby assured me he would arrange the posting. He did.

So off I went to 4 Group where one of my duties was to go to one of the stations in the group when operations were taking place, listen to the briefing and be there at the debriefing when the aircraft returned to base. The amusing thing was that I had been given the permanent award of the Pathfinder Badge and No. 4 Group was a main force group, where the aircrew always loved to claim that something was wrong with the Pathfinder marking.

They loved it even more when they saw someone wearing the Pathfinder Badge at one of their debriefings. Mind you, I got some fun out of it when crews claimed to have bombed on the target indicators which had not been accurately placed and when they were asked which colour of target indicator they had used as an aiming point they calmly said that they had bombed on a certain colour which was the cancellation colour of the operation. The real target indicators were of a specific colour and if any of them were wide of the aiming point they were cancelled by the dropping of other indicators which meant 'Do not bomb on this indicator.'

The 4 Group headquarters in York were in Heslington Hall and the Air Officer commanding the group was the famous Gus Walker, in his time a brilliant rugby player and referee and also a first-class airman. We got on very well together, not only during my stay with 4 Group but after the war as well.

It was because of Gus Walker that I would have been happy to stay at 4 Group for the remainder of the war, but that wasn't to be. The officer who was being posted to the Far East and whose place I had taken, was found unfit so he returned to 4 Group. It was suggested that I should go to the Far East instead, but Lord Willoughby scotched that. He told me that he didn't think I should be posted out East after all the flying I had done.

He asked me how I would like to go and work with John Macadam. Now there was a magical name! John Macadam was one of the top sports journalists in Fleet Street before he joined the RAF, and bearing in mind my ambitions in that direction I jumped at the chance although I had no idea where he was working. Lord Willoughby told me that John was the chief public relations officer with the RAF side of the First Allied Airborne Army. That is where I went to join him.

Working with John Macadam was a sheer delight. He was a down-to-earth Scot, a brilliant writer and a member of the distinguished team of sports journalists the *Daily Express* had at the time. Those were the days when the *Daily Express* outsold all the other newspapers, and with due respect to those who worked in other departments, it was largely due to the paper's excellent sports coverage.

There was Trevor Wignall, a giant of the trade, a man who could report on all sports but whose first love was boxing. A fiercely patriotic Welshman, he never let his nationality cloud his vision. When the great Welsh heavyweight, Tommy Farr, who put Tonypandy on the map, was matched against Joe Louis, the American who seemed capable of destroying almost anyone he fought, Wignall sensibly tipped Louis to win. The blue riband of boxing, the heavyweight championship of the world, was not, according to Trevor Wignall, going to Wales.

That incensed the Welsh, but not half as much as Trevor's post-bout report. The world and his wife had expected Farr to receive the walloping of his life and be counted out before the contest had reached even the fringe of half-time. But Tommy Farr fought the fight of his life and although he lost the bout, he won the respect of the boxing world, and even the respect of people who didn't follow boxing.

Many Welsh people thought Farr had won the fight, but that was the heart leading the head. Trevor Wignall reported he thought Louis was a good winner, and for that his fellow

Welshmen burned his effigy on a huge bonfire. When you can stir emotions like that then you are a writer of power.

Up in the North, in Manchester, there was Henry Rose, the man who carefully and generously guided my first steps in sports journalism. He seemed to read everything I wrote and when I graduated to radio and television, he must have listened and watched because he would regularly send me notes, some of them congratulatory if my work deserved them, others of criticism if I hadn't come up to scratch. If I may borrow a phrase out of a well-known BBC series of yesteryear, I would not have got where I am today without the help and encouragement of Henry Rose.

Henry came from Norwich. He used to say that Norwich was famous only for Mr Colman and for Henry Rose. His career, though, blossomed in South Wales, where he began as copy boy for Hugh Cudlipp. He loved publicity, believing that any publicity was good for him and for his newspaper. He would tip hotel page boys to get an announcement made asking for 'Henry Rose of the *Daily Express* to report to reception.' You could guarantee that when you stepped off the train at Cardiff en route to an international at Ninian Park an announcement would ask 'Henry Rose, of the *Daily Express* to go to the station master's office.' Notice that Henry always insisted on 'Henry Rose of the *Daily Express*' and not just 'Henry Rose'.

He enjoyed making forecasts but couldn't stand giving pools forecasts in the paper. The *Express* sports staff were called upon each week to forecast either three draws, four aways or what-have-you. Henry hated it. One week he selected the only four away wins on the coupon. I telephoned my congratulations to him and after thanking me he added, 'But I haven't won anything. I didn't do the pools but when the editor asked for my four away wins I just gave him the four digits in my telephone number.'

Henry loved to make outrageous predictions. On the morning of the 1938 FA Cup Final between Huddersfield Town and Preston North End he announced that the game would end in a goalless draw after extra time. No Wembley final had ever gone into extra time or ended in a draw, goalless or otherwise, so the odds against Henry's forecast being right were almost astronomical. But he was ALMOST right. Preston won 1–0 but only with a penalty kick in the very last minute of extra time.

Another time Henry forecast that Arsenal would not lose another match, cup or league. They were already in the cup final so Henry forecast wins all the way in the league. On the afternoon of his forecast I sat next to Henry in the press box at Bloomfield Road ground, Blackpool, where Arsenal were playing. After twenty minutes the score was Blackpool 3, Arsenal 0.

The spectators were having great fun at Henry's expense and one fan turned to the press box and invited Henry to 'Come and have a cup of tea with me and forget all about your forecast.' Henry turned to me and said, 'Just think how many extra people will buy the paper on Monday to see how I get out of this.'

When Henry Rose was killed in the Munich air crash in 1958, journalism lost a real stalwart. On the day of his funeral Manchester came to a standstill. I was one of his countless friends waiting on the steps of the *Daily Express* offices in Great Ancoats Street for the cortège to arrive and pause at the place where Henry would like his soul to rest. We had all bought hats for the funeral because Henry was Jewish. As the hearse turned into Great Ancoats Street I asked Lou Gelder, one of Henry's Jewish friends, whether I should keep my hat off, put it on and keep it on, or put it on and then remove it when the coffin finally arrived.

Henry Rose would have loved the reply: 'Kenneth, why don't

you Gentiles behave like Gentiles and let us Jews behave like Jews?'

It was a long journey from Great Ancoats Street to Southern Cemetery, and a very moving one as well. People packed the pavement on both sides of the road to pay their last respects to a popular figure. Offices and factories emptied so that the work people could be part of the funeral. And Desmond Hackett, the man Henry had groomed to succeed him, came out with the remark of the day: 'Henry will be spitting blood up there and demanding to know why there are no contents bills out announcing that Henry Rose is here today.'

Desmond became a formidable character, too, never afraid to take a risk. He made his brown bowler as famous as Eric Morecambe made Ernie Wise's short, fat, hairy legs. Arsenal were one of the first teams, if not the very first, to go to Moscow after the war and play Moscow Dynamo. Des made the trip before anyone else and watched Dynamo play on the Sunday. So the early editions of the *Daily Express* on the morning of the big match carried a front page story by Desmond Hackett who described how when the Arsenal team disembarked at Moscow Airport he was the only English journalist there and was able to doff his brown bowler and tell Tom Whittaker, the Arsenal manager, the strengths and weaknesses of the Moscow Dynamo side.

The story was dropped from later editions when a news flash from Reuters reported that due to fog in Moscow, the aircraft carrying the Arsenal team was diverted to Leningrad, as it was then called.

But back to John Macadam. Like all good Scots he enjoyed a few drams of that wonderful Scottish drink and often he would arrive at the office from the Press Club a little under the weather. He would doze over his typewriter unless he was roused and asked for his copy. Then he would wake up, pound out his deathless prose on the typewriter and return to the Press Club.

Once he fumed at a sub-editor who ruined his opening line of a report on a football match which ended in a dull, goalless draw. John had written, 'This was much ado about nothing . . . nothing.' The sub-editor, who perhaps had never heard of William Shakespeare, changed it to, 'This was much ado about nil-nil.'

My favourite of all the John Macadam pieces was the one about the Glaswegian who was on his way home when he came to a greyhound track. The temptation proved too great for him, so he went inside and with his last five shillings (this is an old money story!) backed the rank outsider. It won at 20–1. Feeling rich with £5.5s. (for the younger reader that is £5.25p) he had another flutter and risked it all on the no. 3 dog, which obliged at 8–1. Flushed with success he put the whole lot on a 6–1 shot. In it came.

By now he was convinced this was his night so he decided to go carefully. He fancied the favourite at 2–1, and it won by a couple of lengths. He decided to go for a real gamble on race number five and put everything he had on a 7–1 shot which the formbook said was prone to run wide. It ran high, wide and handsome and just pipped the favourite in a photo-finish.

Three races left and our Scottish friend had to go round the track and spread his bets. He backed the same dog but with every bookie he could find and his fancy did the business and was a winner at 5–1. Up £47,628 on the night our friend decided to risk it all on the second favourite in race seven. It came up trumps at 2–1.

One race to go, and £142,884 up on the night. This was his birthday and Christmas rolled into one.

He was sweating as he had never sweated before. He visited every bookmaker putting as much as the bookie would take on the redhot favourite. The dog had never been beaten and he was being offered at 3–1 on, although some bookmakers were reluctant to take any more money for him.

Our fearless punter couldn't bear to watch the race so he just stood behind the stand. He didn't like the cheering he heard at the end and walked to see the results board and the starting prices. The favourite had been beaten for the very first time. He shrugged his shoulders and began the long walk home. He was glad he hadn't watched his £142,884 go down the drain.

When he got home, his wife had just put the kettle on to boil. She asked him if he would like a cup of tea and he said he would. Then the conversation went like this:

WIFE: 'Where did you go tonight?'
HIM: 'Oh, I just looked in at the dog track.'
WIFE: 'Have a good time?'
HIM: 'Yeah.'
WIFE: 'Lose much?'
HIM: 'No. Only five bob.'

Only John Macadam could think up a story like that, but it was typical of the man to make up a joke story to put across to his readers the serious point that gambling is a game where punters lose and bookmakers win.

7

Norway Liberated

John Macadam and I were based in Virginia Water, a beautiful part of the country not far from Windsor or from those wonderful golf courses at Sunningdale and Wentworth . . . although I didn't play the game at the time, not having recovered from Alf Groves' criticism at St Andrews.

It was the first time I had ever served in an inter-service unit but I soon got used to it. I commuted between Virginia Water and the airfield we used at Earls Colne in Essex. It was a great surprise a few years ago when Eddie Shah invited me to take part in the William Roach's (*Coronation Street*'s Ken Barlow) Golf Classic at his excellent Essex Golf & Country Club to find that I would be playing golf right next to Earls Colne airfield, which is now used as a flying school.

Once upon a time it was the nerve centre of one of the biggest airborne operations of the Second World War – the crossing of the Rhine. And the world's press was there to witness it as it happened. I was designated to look after two or three of the war correspondents, with particular attention being paid to an American gentleman from CBS (Columbia Broadcasting System). His name was Ed Murrow.

His name and his voice were well known to everyone in the

United Kingdom because he had been in our midst throughout the war. He was the man who used to stroll through the streets of London at the height of the blitz chatting to the citizens and getting their views on tape for his nightly report to the United States. It took the form of a letter to Hitler which Murrow always began with the greeting, 'Dear Mr Schicklgrüber' which was Adolf Hitler's real name.

The final briefing for the press was attended by the Director of Public Relations, who wished everybody good luck and added, 'As you join our armed forces flying east into danger I shall be flying west on a pleasant trip to the United States. And I shall be keeping my fingers crossed for the 100 per cent success of the operation.'

Ed Murrow had a reputation for always asking the final question at briefings and he lived up to it on this occasion. He wanted to know how long the embargo on news of the operation would be in force and who would eventually make the announcement. He was assured that official news of the operation would be released at the same time in London and Paris. Being an old hand at the game Ed Murrow was suspicious and he struck a £5 bet that Paris would break the embargo and give the news to the world before London. The Director of Public Relations accepted the bet and said that he was confident that he would be £5 richer and Ed Murrow would be £5 poorer.

The operation was a huge success – the lessons of Arnhem had been learned – and, sure enough, Paris broke the embargo. So Ed Murrow won his bet, but he never received his £5 because we who had flown east to danger all got back safely, having delivered the troops to the other side of the River Rhine, but the civilian Director of Public Relations, who was flying west on a pleasant trip to the United States, was neither seen nor heard of again. The aircraft was presumed lost over the Atlantic.

The advance through Germany went on until May when the Prime Minister announced over the wireless that the following day would be VE Day, Victory in Europe Day. I was driving through Leicester Square with three colleagues when a civilian, eyes focused only on the news in the four-page evening paper, stepped into the road. Our driver jammed on his brakes, wound the window down and shouted to the jaywalker, 'I know the news is good, my old friend, but don't get yourself killed reading it.'

The four of us realized that the West End bars would be full to bursting point so we decided that the Air Ministry was the place to go. We drove down Haymarket easily enough but as we turned into Trafalgar Square *en route* for Whitehall there was chaos. People were dancing and singing and they were in no mood to make way for a car.

So we all put on our uniform hats and looked businesslike as a senior-looking policeman came towards us. Our driver told him, 'Officer, we know there's a lot to celebrate but the war isn't over yet. The fighting is still going on in the Far East and the Japanese are a long way from being beaten. It's essential we get to a meeting in the Air Ministry.'

The policeman was suitably impressed even though I was the only passenger in the car with a flying badge on my uniform. And not just the pilot's wings, but the Pathfinder Badge (which was now well known to the public) and the Bar, which I had recently been awarded, to my Distinguished Flying Cross.

No doubt thinking that we were on our way to meet with the War Cabinet, the police officer got his troops together: a couple of mounted policemen rode in front of us and two policemen walked on either side of the car as we inched our way forward through the massed throng. Seeing four RAF officers in the car, the crowd cheered and waved and blew kisses as if we had just beaten the Nazis all on our own.

It must have taken us a good twenty-five minutes to get down Whitehall and reach the turning into the Air Ministry. When we got there we parked the car and hurried to our important meeting, which took place in the bar.

After the celebrations I was ordered to fly to Oslo to take part in the liberation of the country. That was something of a joke because by the time we got there the Norwegians had risen and done the job themselves. But we landed at an airfield called Gardemoen, some thirty miles to the north of Oslo, and proceeded into the capital by lorry. The troops were in the back while I sat in the front with the driver. The people gave us a wonderful welcome, which was a bit of a surprise because we knew the Norwegians felt that we could have helped them more when they were invaded. But they had obviously forgotten their resentment and they clapped, cheered and blew kisses.

Not, I am afraid, to the front of the lorry. I got scowls, not a few shaken fists and a thoroughly unwelcome welcome, if you follow my meaning. The Norwegian driver told me not to worry. He explained that my RAF blue uniform looked very similar to a German officer's uniform and the people lining the streets thought I was a German prisoner. All I can say is that once the Norwegians realized I was not German their welcome and friendship knew no bounds.

Norway was a place of great excitement after the liberation. Quisling, whose name has become synonymous with 'traitor', had been arrested but there were stories that the Hermann Goering regiment had taken to the mountains and was planning a guerrilla war. Then it was said that the German commander-in-chief had not been apprehended. He was later, rumour has it, found living in the Hotel Bristol, where we were staying.

What was known for certain was that many supporters of the traitor Quisling were still at large and armed. We were all, therefore, ordered to carry revolvers, which was something new for an ex-pilot. I soon realized how necessary the precaution was because almost every night one could hear the sounds of gun battles, some of them quite close.

But most people were cheered by the news that Crown Prince Olav was on his way home. He had sailed from Scotland and was being escorted by Royal Navy minesweepers. As the convoy neared Norway it was announced in the newspapers that once the Crown Prince had disembarked the ships would be open to the public.

The morning after the Crown Prince's arrival a friend and I walked down to the quayside, which is just about in the centre of the city. Frankly we were running short of cigarettes, drink and any other luxuries you could think of and we thought the Royal Navy would be obliging. It was not yet nine o'clock in the morning but the place was alive with joyful Norwegians. We wanted to board one of the minesweepers to see the radar officer – hoping like hell there was one – and we fought our way through the throng. As we approached the gangway I reminded my friend that we would be piped aboard and would have to salute the quarterdeck the moment we stepped on board. We asked to see the radar officer and a rating was told to take us to the wardroom. I was surprised at how small it was but then the complement of the minesweeper did not include many officers. Nor did it include the beautiful Norwegian girls who were there being entertained by the Royal Navy officers.

We had a splendid time on board and were plied with cigarettes, drink, fruit and chocolate. You name it and we were given it. The officers told us they had sailed from Scotland to Oslo and were going straight back to Scotland although they had stocked up for a long cruise. They were due to leave the following morning and we were invited to come and collect some more goodies.

As we were leaving one of the ratings asked me where I came from. I told him Salford, in Lancashire, and by coincidence he came from the same place. He offered to telephone my family and tell them I was safe and well in Oslo, which he did when he landed back in the UK.

We went down the next morning to say goodbye, and witnessed the crowds waving and cheering as the ships began to move while the crews of the minesweepers played their part by throwing cigarettes, fruit and chocolate to their well-wishers.

Life was much more pleasant after meeting up with the Navy. We had plenty of little luxuries to keep us going, and then we found out that there were regular service flights out of Oslo to Copenhagen. We took advantage of those because they gave us the opportunity of having the most wonderful bacon and eggs at Kastrup, the airport of the Danish capital.

The Norwegians went out of their way to make us feel at home, and they even had the nerve to take me to the top of the famous Olympic Games ski jump tower at Holmenkollen. For someone who cannot stand heights it was not a pleasant experience. Nor was it a pleasant experience to be taken to the concentration camp at Grini. Seeing some of the instruments of torture there, it was hard to believe that people could be so cruel to other human beings.

Oslo itself is a city of rare beauty. The harbour landing stage comes almost to the centre of the city and the approach to the harbour up the Oslo fjord is an experience that can never be forgotten. The Norwegians are justly proud of their National Theatre and it was there that I sat through the whole performance of *Peer Gynt* . . . in Norwegian.

The main street is Karl Johanns Gate, which the British troops quickly translated into Charlie Jones Street. It is flanked by some lovely gardens and at the top is the royal palace. The Crown Prince and Princess were in residence waiting for the big day of celebration – 17 May, Norway's National Day – when Norwegians celebrate their independence from Sweden. How fitting that it should come just over a week after their liberation from Nazi Germany.

It was a day of great rejoicing which opened with a huge parade up Charlie Jones Street to the royal palace. Everyone took part, the Norwegian services, the members of the Resistance (the Hjemme Fronten) and the British forces, not forgetting the ordinary citizens who had played their part during the occupation. The bands performed continually and the favourite pieces of music were the national anthem, *Ja Vi Elskar Dette Landet* (Yes, We Love This Land), and what we took to be our national anthem. The music certainly was the same and some of the Norwegians sang 'God Save the King' for our benefit, but really the Norwegians recognized the music as that for their own King's Song.

The long, enjoyable day was followed in the evening by a huge ball in the Hotel Bristol. Everybody who was anybody was there, including some of the loveliest ladies you could wish to see. We had heard a lot about the beauty of the Scandinavian women but this was way above our expectations. Obviously there was a lot of competition to dance with the most beautiful ones and with a few RAF lads there the line-shooting was terrific. 'Shooting a line' was a national sport in the RAF. It was a form of boasting which was quite acceptable and every station had its own 'Line Book' in which the 'lines' were recorded, with the 'line shooter' given the credit while those who had heard the 'line' appended their names as witnesses.

One could fill a whole book with classic lines, so here are just a few to whet your appetite. There was, for instance, a pilot who ditched in the sea on two of his first three operational flights. When a new member of the squadron entered the Mess for the first time he was greeted by the said pilot with, 'Hello, my name's Skinner but they all call me Swimmer.' He was last heard of on his next (fourth) operation sending out a Mayday call when over the North Sea.

Then there was the old one, usually told at debriefings by pilots who had been on a low-level flight. 'We had a miraculous escape. We almost collided with a U-Boat that was surfacing.'

Even the administrative staff didn't escape, hence the inclusion of an accounts officer in the line book, claiming, 'I've been working like a black all day.' That from a nine-to-five lad! (There was no such thing as political incorrectness in those days.)

But enough of the line-shooting, of which I did my share at the Hotel Bristol that night. Campaign medals had by now been handed out and as well as the Distinguished Flying Cross and Bar there were such things as the 1938 Star and a few more which escape my memory. The lovely lady with whom I was dancing asked what all my ribbons stood for, and she was intrigued when I told her that the highest award was on the extreme right under the flying badge and the others followed in decreasing order of importance. The charming young Norwegian lady pointed to my first medal ribbon and asked loudly, while nodding to someone behind me, 'Is your most important ribbon higher than his?'

As I turned to see who was behind me I heard a voice say, 'Of course it is, my dear.' I was standing face-to-face with Brigadier General Smythe, who smiled and danced away. His most important medal was 'only' the Victoria Cross!

My tour of duty in Oslo came to an end just after 17 May but by this time I had heard that the RAF Exhibition, currently in Copenhagen, would be moving to Oslo. I thought to myself, that is just the job for me: officer in charge of the RAF Exhibition in Norway. So as soon as I got back to London I went to the Air Ministry and got confirmation that the exhibition really was going to move to Oslo. There and then I told them I had all the qualifications needed such as ability to speak Norwegian and experience during the war. Believe it or not, I kept my face straight all the time I was shooting that line.

Anyway, I got the job and the first thing I was handed was a mountainous list of captions which needed translating from English to Norwegian. 'No problem at all,' I assured them, and walked out of the Air Ministry and straight into Norway House. There I told them the truth, the whole truth and nothing but the truth, that I had just got back from Norway and had volunteered for the job of officer in charge of the RAF Exhibition in Oslo. They plied me with questions about the people at home, how they were, whether everything was all right, and when I said that I had been to Grini they asked me all about it. They were so happy at the liberation and that the Crown Prince had received a wonderful welcome and 17 May had been celebrated just as 17 May should be.

I showed them the captions and they were only too willing to do the translations for me. So, I thanked them all profusely for their help, handed over the captions and went home to Salford for a week.

8

My Generosity Goes Unappreciated

The RAF Exhibition created much interest in Oslo and great excitement for all of us RAF personnel who were working on it when the news was announced that the Crown Prince and Princess would perform the opening ceremony. There was a large crowd in the square outside the Christana Glasmagasin where the exhibition was held, and some of us were a wee bit twitchy until it was all over because Quisling had been sentenced to death and some of his supporters who were still at large had made it known that if he died King Haakon would be assassinated. Happily, though, the opening went off peacefully and we settled down to greet the big crowds which flocked in every day.

There was a lot for them to see, such as pictures of the bombing at home and also of the RAF's bombing raids and destruction caused in Germany. There was a meteorological set which provided up-to-day weather forecasts every day and the most popular exhibit was a large model of a Lancaster, perfect in every detail.

Then we got the news that King Haakon, who by this time

had arrived home, would be visiting the exhibition. Bearing in mind the threat made by Quisling's supporters, who were still causing sporadic shootings in the streets at night, I was surprised when the date and time of the King's visit were published, but it was made clear that the public would not be allowed into the exhibition during the King's visit.

I could not help thinking that if the worst did happen and the King was killed, the repercussions would be monumental. None of the senior officers would admit to being at fault. The police and security people would claim that they had overlooked nothing and had taken every precaution that was necessary. That left one person – me.

Yes, the buck would stop with me and I would be held responsible for the death of a very popular monarch. I began to wonder whether I would be shot at dawn or sentenced to life imprisonment or expelled from Norway with orders never to return.

Happily there was no attempt on the King's life, in fact no demonstrations at all. On the contrary, the huge crowds which had assembled in the square long before the King was due to arrive went wild with joy when his car drew up outside the entrance.

King Haakon was a charming man, interesting to talk to and interested in everything he saw. The first thing he wanted to look at was the weather forecast which said that the rain which had started would not last and that sunny weather would follow. To this day I can remember him smiling and saying, 'Young man, I am a seafaring man and those of us who go to sea know the weather. Now the weather here in Oslo isn't going to change until the wind direction changes and there is no mention of a wind change in the weather report.'

Yes, he knew his stuff, did King Haakon. Later that day the

wind changed and so did the weather. Eat your heart out, Michael Fish!

A lovely souvenir of the day were the photos taken of us which both King Haakon and the Crown Prince were kind enough to autograph.

I thought that we had survived the royal visits but soon learned that there was another one to come. Crown Prince Olav's two children had arrived home after spending the war years in the safety of Canada, and they were anxious to visit the exhibition. So I was there to greet Prince Harald (now King of Norway) and his sister, who were accompanied by their nanny. Like their father and grandfather they were interested in everything they saw.

I was careful to address the royal children as Your Royal Highnesses, and the nanny kept ordering the children to 'Say "Sir" to the officer.' It became almost laughable. My 'Would Your Royal Highnesses like to see how the weather reports are compiled?' would produce the eager reply in a heavy Canadian accent of 'Oh, yes please', followed by an authoritarian 'Say "Sir" to the officer'. This brought forth a quick, 'Oh, yes please, sir' in their best Canadian.

Eventually we reached the model of the Lancaster. Prince Harald's eyes lit up and there was a cry of 'Gee,' followed by a quick second thought of 'Sir'. I told him all about the aircraft, showing him how the undercarriage worked, how the bomb doors opened and closed and I had an audience of one royal prince in raptures. He obviously would have been happy to spend the rest of the day with the Lancaster, so I said, 'Would Your Royal Highness like to have this model?' His eyes shone as he replied, 'Gee, yes I would . . . sir.'

I turned to two airmen and said, 'Take this model to the royal car, please,' and they did.

The visit over we stood at the door and I said to Prince Harald, 'I hope you have a lot of fun with the model Lancaster at the palace, Your Royal Highness.' He shook my hand and said, 'Yes we will, sir. Thank you very much, sir.' He had obviously got into the rhythm of the day. The Princess thanked me and then the nanny shook my hand and said, 'Thank you. You have been very kind, sir.' There was quite an emphasis on that last 'sir'.

I couldn't wait to get a signal off to the Air Ministry. I told the powers-that-be that Prince Harald had taken such a liking to the model of the Lancaster that I had presented it to him in the cause of Anglo-Norwegian friendship. Everyone in the exhibition thought it was a marvellous gesture and the Norwegians were as happy as the proverbial Larry.

I didn't get an immediate reply from the Air Ministry to my signal so I assumed they were discussing what high honour they could bestow on me for doing such a splendid job for my country's relationship with an ally. I thought of a knighthood or perhaps a peerage and I was perfectly willing to accept either . . . or both.

Then I got the reply. There was no knighthood, no peerage, in fact there was sweet fanny adams except for an over-sized rocket. Apparently the model was the only one of its kind in the world. (All the more reason, I would have thought, for presenting it to the grandson of the King of one of our staunchest allies.) It belonged to A. V. Roe & Co., the makers of the Lancaster, and they had only agreed to loan it to the RAF for the purpose of the exhibition on the condition that it was returned to them unharmed in any way.

No one had told me this when I took over the exhibition (or if they had I wasn't listening) and quite frankly I am sure that A. V. Roe & Co., would be delighted to know that their wonderful model was now in the royal palace in Oslo, giving great pleasure to Prince Harald and, I am sure, to his dad and grandad. I was also convinced that the wonderful company of A. V. Roe, which built a few thousand or so Lancaster bombers, could manage to turn out another model to make up for the one I had given away.

I often wonder whether they ever did. And I often wonder whether the model is still in the royal palace at the top of Charlie Jones Street in Oslo.

We had a super party when the exhibition closed although I had made a strict resolution that I would not drink any more of that vile German cheap brandy that was doing the rounds. I had learned my lesson at a party at an air base outside Oslo where this firewater (that is the only fair description for the stuff) was flowing thick and fast. When I woke up the next morning I felt like death. The batman came in and told me he had experienced the evil effects himself and he knew the remedy. He brought me a cup of very sweet tea with milk (when the only way I drink tea is with no milk or sugar) and told me to get it down. It made me feel a hundred times worse.

Eventually I got up, shaved and showered and struggled into the Mess. Fortunately I bumped into one of the medical officers and I told him the whole sorry story. He was well aware of the symptoms and when I mentioned the batman's cure he shook his head. 'Young man,' he said, 'you must drink no liquid for twenty-four hours, nor eat any fruit because of the juices.' He warned me that one small drink of water would send me back on the road to oblivion. I then embarked on the most horrible, painful twenty-four hours I have ever experienced.

That is why I wanted none of the dreadful brandy at the party. And that is why it was such a fine party. Everyone had brought along some friends and towards the end of the celebrations I told the flight sergeant, who was the senior NCO on the staff, that my friends and I were going along to the officers' club. He was a very responsible fellow so I told him to remember to lock up the place before he left and to make sure he was the last to leave.

When I got back to England I was due for demobilization, but I was told that the exhibition had arrived back at Leith in a Polish destroyer with certain things missing. My demobilization would have to be delayed until Special Branch had finished their investigation. I knew the officers who were investigating and I asked them what was missing. Nothing of any real value, they said, just some badges and things like that.

They thought it would be better if they made another trip to Oslo but I have very good idea that it was a pleasure rather than a business trip. Not that I blame them. The final report stated that nothing of any real value was missing, and what was missing had, no doubt, been taken by people as souvenirs. To make matters even more complicated, there was a dock strike on at Leith when the Polish destroyer arrived, although I cannot imagine a Leith docker or a Polish deckhand wanting an RAF badge as a souvenir.

My stay in Scandinavia was not confined to Norway. I also spent a lot of time in Denmark. The bacon and egg restaurant at Kastrup airport was the great attraction in Copenhagen, but I had a chance meeting with a gentleman who took myself and a friend to Belle Vue, a lovely resort outside the Danish capital. It was a hot day and he suggested we have a drink of schnapps. Why I don't know, but I associated schnapps with Schweppes, that refreshing fizzy drink we knew at home. I was, therefore, bewildered to be handed a small glass of colourless liquid and told to drink it in one gulp to the toast of 'din skol, min skol, alle vackre flike skol', or in English, 'Your health, my health, all the pretty girls' health.' Far from being a cooling and refreshing fizzy drink it was a very, very strong drink – Danish aquavit. Apparently the correct way to drink it is with Danish lager, one gulp of iced aquavit and then one mouthful of lager.

It was in Copenhagen that I was invited to a party where I met a very attractive lady who told me her husband, who would soon be arriving, was the sports editor of the afternoon newspaper, *B.T.* It was then that I met Ralf Buch, one of the most respected journalists in Denmark. We became very friendly and I wrote a number of articles for his newspaper. The Danish pools also used a few English matches so Ralf asked me to forecast the results of these games each week. Sadly I have never been a good forecaster so I never made any Dane a millionaire.

But I enjoyed the summer of 1945, the summer in which I got married, most of which I spent in Norway and Denmark. The following year my wife and I went to stay with the Buchs and we had a wonderful holiday party in Copenhagen and partly on the island of Fyn, where we met a famous artist who loved eating strawberries but who covered them with Danish lager instead of cream. There is no accounting for taste.

9

Hello Radio

I ended my career in the RAF by achieving a dream. I had always wanted to fly in a Sunderland flying boat, one of those large, sturdy aircraft that used to spend hours patrolling the Atlantic Ocean searching for U-boats and other enemy shipping. I was only a passenger, but it was a memorable experience as we chugged ever so slowly from Oslo to Calshot. We got there in the end and I was then taught a lesson on how to be careful about HM Customs and Excise.

We had brought with us the usual amount of alcohol and cigarettes, and furs were also a popular buy in Norway. I had a silver fox fur for my wife and the customs people were happy to accept that. But in the train on the way from Calshot to London, one of the officers in the compartment was proud (and stupid) enough to tell us that he had brought in more than his allowance of alcohol and tobacco and he also had with him half a dozen furs.

Another gentleman in the compartment leaned forward and said to him, 'Take a tip from me and never talk about it if you have brought into the country more than your entitlement and not told the customs officer because you can always be apprehended and charged afterwards. I know because I happen

77

to be a senior customs officer. I'm not going to report you this time but remember that just as careless talk cost lives during the war, careless talk can also cost you a lot of money in peacetime if you have defrauded the Customs and Excise.'

I made a resolution to give up smuggling for good.

Back in England, and with the inquiry into the losses from the exhibition now finished, I was able to bow out of the RAF and start my demobilization leave. The year was a good one because Bolton Wanderers had reached the semi-final of the FA Cup and they were due to play Charlton Athletic at Villa Park, the home of Aston Villa.

I thought to myself, you must go to Villa Park. I wrote to the Football Association pointing out that I was a pre-war sports writer (the fact that my journalistic career had lasted a full six months as a general reporter on a local weekly newspaper had nothing to do with the Football Association, had it?) and a former bomber pilot now on demobilization leave, so could I please have a press ticket for the semi-final at Villa Park. It was the cheekiest letter I have ever written and anyone trying on the same thing today would wait for ever for a reply. But I got not only a reply but also a press ticket. I could not believe my luck.

I had never been to Villa Park before in my life and I couldn't wait to get there. When I did, I stood in the press box and looked round what even in those days was a superb stadium compared with most of its rivals. I was taking it all in, savouring the experience, when I heard a voice say, 'Good gracious, what the hell are you doing here?' I recognized the voice immediately and as I turned towards the sound I knew I was right. There he was, standing in front of me, my friend the timekeeper from Sywell during the war. But he was no longer logging Tiger Moths out and logging them back in again. He was now the sports editor of the *Sunday Empire News*. His name was Harold Mayes.

We chatted away and Harold asked me what I was going to do. I told him I wanted to get into journalism properly so I would go out into the big, wide world and chance my luck. We swapped telephone numbers and a few days afterwards I got a call from Harold and he uttered the words which changed my whole world. He just said, 'Would you do 300 words on League Cricket for the *Empire News*?'

League Cricket was very big in Lancashire and the two biggest leagues were the Lancashire League and the Central Lancashire League. Towns such as Accrington, Burnley, Colne, Milnrow, Nelson, Radcliffe, Rochdale and many others had their own teams and they were well supported. As well as the local players, the clubs had one professional and at one time, for instance, Nelson had the magnificent Learie Constantine as their pro. When the war ended there was a great influx of overseas stars such as the West Indies formidable trio of Walcott, Weekes and Worrall.

But all that was to come so I had to rack my brain to try and find out something about league cricket. Then I received a letter from Worsley Cricket Club. I had been a junior member there before the war and they wrote to me (and lots of other people) because they were celebrating their centenary. Strictly speaking, Worsley didn't play league cricket. They were members of the Manchester Association and, unlike clubs in the Lancashire and Central Lancashire Leagues, they did not allow professionals. That didn't really matter. It was Worsley's centenary and I had been given full details about their history and how they were going to celebrate the great occasion. That was enough for my 300-word piece, which I ended with the statement that Worsley were 'perhaps the oldest cricket club in the North of England'. It was a ludicrous statement because cricket was a lot older than 100 years, but what did it matter? It mattered even less when I received a telephone call from the BBC North Region offices which were then in Piccadilly, Manchester. They were trying to find the oldest cricket club in the North and asked me to go along to see a man called Victor Smythe.

That was a real breakthrough and I couldn't get to the Piccadilly offices quickly enough, and it was there I met Victor Smythe, who was in charge of all Outside Broadcasts and sport.

Victor Smythe was one of the foundation stones of the BBC. He had joined the organization when it was originally called the British Broadcasting Company and he appeared to know everybody who was anybody in the North of England. He loved racing, he loved show business (it was he who produced shows like *Workers' Playtime* which were so popular then) and he was a giant of a man in every sense. We took to each other straight away and I became a regular in the Friday night sports programme which was broadcast to the North of England.

Before very long, Victor asked if I would like to try my hand at commentary work. Wouldn't I just! And so it came to pass that I was booked to commentate on one day of the game at the Scarborough Cricket Festival between H. G. Leveson-Gower's XI and the touring New Zealanders. The transmission was planned for ten past two until half past on the North Region only. This would have been fine for a county championship match where play resumes after lunch at ten past two. But the Scarborough Festival was a fun event and play didn't start until midday. Lunch was taken at two o'clock until two forty, so there was I destined to give my very first commentary when there was no action.

I was told that if I dried up I could hand back to the studio and they would play some gramophone records, which was the BBC's remedy for any crisis in those early days. I had no intention of drying up. Opportunities like the one I had been given didn't come every day. On the big day, Victor Smythe went into Mrs Mac's, the pub which used to exist in a little alley just round the corner from Broadcasting House in Manchester, and had one scotch. When offered another he declined, saying, 'I must get back. I've got a new commentator doing his first commentary during the luncheon interval of a cricket match.'

Oblivious to all the worries that were besetting people in Broadcasting House, Manchester, I started to talk away in Scarborough, describing what had gone on since the midday start. At the Scarborough Festival there were always many marquees and I described how one had in front of it 'a beautiful bed of tulips in the colours of the MCC'. Now I have never known the first thing about horticulture or plain, down-to-earth gardening so I had not slightest idea that tulips did not bloom at the time of the Scarborough Cricket Festival in September. That sort of information was not in the curriculum at Farnworth Grammar School or the RAF.

The *Yorkshire Post*'s horticultural correspondent really took me to task about my lack of knowledge of things gardening and thundered something along the lines of 'Isn't it time the BBC made sure that its commentators were aware of the simple facts of life?' To this day I have never understood why a knowledge of gardening, however elementary, is considered necessary to do a sporting commentary.

Victor Smythe, on the other had, was delighted. He thought I had done a good job and, being an experienced gentleman of the entertainment industry, said, 'Kenneth, you are on the first rung of the ladder. They have given you publicity in a famous newspaper and they have spelt your name correctly. That is all that matters.'

Commentating on the Scarborough Cricket Festival was fun.

So, too, was commentating on the Bradford League Cup Final. But my ambition was to become a challenger to Raymond Glendenning, who was the football commentator-in-chief. Raymond was a tremendous fellow and although many people criticized him – criticizing radio or television commentators seems to be a national sport in Great Britain – he was a true professional who handled football, racing and boxing. Perhaps he was called upon to cover too much, but he showed his true professionalism when he had to do the commentary on a wartime international at Elland Road, Leeds.

Sadly the day dawned foggy and there seemed little chance of the fog lifting. The game, however, had to go on for security reasons. It would be a breach of security if any inkling of the weather was leaked to the Germans, and the cancellation of a football match would constitute such a breach. Raymond had to do the commentary. The trouble was that he could see hardly anything. He couldn't, for instance, see either set of goalposts. But, without once making a mention of the weather, and making it up as he went along, Raymond produced a brilliant piece of work. I can't help feeling that sometimes we made a meal about security issues. Once a bomber station was put on alert the public telephone lines were cut off so no one could use the ordinary telephone to make calls into or out of the station. It seemed to me that all a German spy had to do was to find out which bomber stations were on stand-by to operate that night was telephone the stations in his area. If he got no answer the bombers were getting ready for action.

Similarly with the football match in Leeds. I am sure the enemy knew what the weather was like in the United Kingdom.

Obviously competing with Raymond Glendenning was going to be no easy matter, but I was delighted to hear that I was to get a chance. Victor Smythe telephoned me and asked me to cover the Third Division (North) game between York City and Stockport County at Bootham Crescent, York. Perhaps it wasn't the most important game in the world of football, but it was a start and it was, let's face it, of paramount importance to the supporters of York City and Stockport County.

We covered the first half with live commentary for the British Forces network, which spread all over the world, and in the second half the national radio network joined us. That was after Victor Smythe, who sat next to me throughout the match, gave me a piece of advice which I happily pass on to any would-be radio commentators, or even to any already well established ones. Victor told me that in the first half I had made a mistake in identifying a player. I had said Smith had the ball and then corrected myself by saying, 'Sorry, it isn't Smith with the ball, it's Jones.'

'Kenneth, you are the eyes of the listener,' said Victor. 'You are their only source of information so they trust you implicitly. But if you admit to a mistake their confidence in you will be dented. The audience will start to lose faith in you. So in future, if you say Smith has got the ball and you suddenly realize that it isn't Smith but Jones, don't apologize. Just let Smith pass the ball to Jones. No one will ever know you have wriggled your way out of an error with a white lie.'

Great advice, but it wouldn't work on television, though! And it was on television that I set my sights when I read that it was restarting in London and the south-east. I say restarting because there was a BBC television service in London before the war.

So many people have forgotten, or never knew, that Great Britain produced the first television service in the world in the late 1930s. Now it had restarted, albeit in a small way, with Alexandra Palace as the nerve centre. I had never seen television because in Manchester we were well out of range of the transmitter and, as we Northerners never tired of saying, according to the BBC, Great Britain ended five miles north of Watford.

Anyway, it was obvious that television was going to become the 'in' thing so I wrote to Mr S. J. De Lotbinière, who was the head of Outside Broadcasts (Radio & Television) – notice that radio was the No. 1 – and told him that I would like to be considered for the job of the BBC's football commentator. Thanks to that letter I was invited to go for an audition at Romford in Essex. There were three other hopefuls there and Mr De Lotbinière told me that no one had any idea about the skills for which they were looking. That did little for my morale, but anyway I did about ten minutes of commentary in each half, as did the other three gentlemen, and I am ashamed to say I cannot remember who Romford were playing that day.

It was a little while before I received any news and this lowered my morale even further, but it transpired that Michael Henderson, the producer and director, had gone into hospital with acute appendicitis the day after the auditions. I was assured the auditions would be rescheduled.

Some little time afterwards the BBC announced the programme for the extension to its television schedules. First they would go into the Midlands, then into the North and so on, and then out of the blue I was asked to go down to Romford once again to commentate on a game. This was not another audition. It was a live outside broadcast of an amateur international trial between the Southern Counties and the Northern Counties at Romford. In other words it was my big chance, my breakthrough.

I wasn't on my own. My co-commentator was a gentleman called Jimmy Jewell, and before you jump to wrong conclusions and wonder why a comedian should be doing a football commentary, I can assure you that this Jimmy Jewell had nothing to do with Ben Warris. He was, in fact, a former referee who had the nerve to award a penalty kick in the last minute of extra time on the 1938 F.A. Cup Final with the score 0–0. Mutch, the Preston inside forward, was brought down by Young, the Huddersfield centre half, picked himself up and scored from the penalty spot to take the cup to Preston.

Jimmy and I worked together for an all too short time, covering mainly amateur games, and then one evening his wife rang me and told me that he had collapsed with a heart attack and died. That was a bitter blow because Jimmy had the makings of an excellent commentator and we got along splendidly together. But his death left the BBC with me, and it was the start of an exciting and wonderful career with BBC television which began in 1948 and, as far as the BBC was concerned, ended in 1971. But more of that later.

10

Welcome to the Magic Lantern

In those very early days television was regarded as the enemy of football and the football authorities claimed that television would be the enemy of all sports. Football coverage was restricted to amateur games and Alan Chivers was the director at all the matches. He kept two notebooks. If we were offered a cup of tea at the end of the game the club would go down in his black book; if we were offered something a wee bit stronger, then the entry would be in the red book, which meant the club was worthy of a further visit. The only professional game we were allowed to cover was the FA Cup Final. The commentary position at Wembley was simply dreadful, well behind the Royal Box. At the critical time of our transmission – ten minutes before the start when the teams were coming on to the field – crowds of people would be walking in front of us trying to find their seats. They were the people who always seem to get Cup Final tickets without ever being supporters of one of the two competing teams.

But as we moved into the 1950s things began to change. More and more countries were joining the television world and the interest in football was increasing. The four home countries had joined FIFA after the war and in 1950 the Home

International Championship between England, Northern Ireland, Scotland and Wales was regarded a qualifying group for the World Cup, with the top two teams out of the four qualifying for the Finals in Brazil. England and Scotland qualified but only England decided to make the trip, whereas Scotland had said they would only go as the British champions. Having finished second they refused to take part.

They were no better four years later when the final stages of the World Cup were televised for the first time. Scotland qualified, again through the Home International Championship, but the Scots were so uninterested that they allowed Rangers to go on a meaningless tour of the United States which meant the squad was seriously depleted. They took just thirteen players to Switzerland and departed after the first round, having lost 1–0 to Austria and then 7–0 to Uruguay. To complete the whole Scottish fiasco, their manager resigned in the middle of the tournament. Thank goodness they have learned the lessons of those years.

The English squad in 1950 under the management of Walter Winterbottom seemed a very strong one, including such players as Tom Finney, Stanley Matthews, Wilf Mannion, Alf Ramsey and Billy Wright, but we got our first inkling of how the game had improved all over the world when we were eliminated in the first round of matches. We even managed to lose to the United States of America 1–0 in Belo Horizonte.

Perhaps our only consolation was that the final match of the 1950 World Cup in which Uruguay beat Brazil in the new Maracana stadium to win the World Cup (as they did in the very first World Cup competition) was refereed by an Englishman, George Reader, of Southampton, who later became chairman of Southampton Football Club.

We could also take some credit for the fact that another

Englishman, George Raynor, was the coach of the Swedish team. In the 1948 Olympic Games in London he led Sweden to the gold medal. Then the professional scouts stripped him of all his best players, but in just two years he rebuilt the team and finished third behind Uruguay and Brazil.

There was a gentleman at the BBC in the early 1950s called Imlay Newbiggin-Watts. I am not sure what his title was or what exactly was his brief, but he seemed to handle a lot of international affairs. If I mentioned to him that a big international was taking place in Europe he would try his hardest to get it shown on BBC television. I was delighted about this; delighted, too, that the BBC had a sports department which, despite the lack of competition because at the time Independent Television had not yet been created, wanted to set the standards for sports broadcasting.

Peter Dimmock was the head of the BBC's sports organization, in fact head of Outside Broadcasts. He was himself a horse-racing enthusiast, but he recognized the pull of football. When the excellent *Sportsview* midweek programme started, Peter introduced it himself, which perhaps was not the right thing to do. The head of a department had to be able to judge the efficiency of his presenters. If he acted as a presenter himself and made any error, however slight, it diluted his right to criticize other presenters. I remember a time when I interviewed Alan Hardaker, then the secretary of the Football League and renowned as one who saw in television a great danger to football. At the end of the interview I gave the football result of a match which settled a promotion duel on goal average. I said the all-important goal average difference was 0.3 of a goal, whereupon Peter immediately picked that up and exclaimed, 'What on earth is 0.3 of a goal? What a ridiculous way to settle an important contest.' And he added something about football's stupidity. Alan Hardaker nearly hit the roof.

Peter Dimmock built up a first-class team that ensured the BBC was *the* sporting network and remained so even after the appearance of Independent Television. Peter's team was headed by Paul Fox, a paratrooper during the war, and a man who made such a success of his career in television that he reached the top at the BBC, then moved to ITV and did the same thing there. He graduated from sport to current affairs when still with the BBC, and stuck with current affairs when he left, although he still had a passion for sport, even going so far as to support Arsenal!

Although I didn't see eye to eye with Paul Fox later on in life and although he was one of the reasons I left the BBC, one cannot help admiring the way he built up the BBC's sports organization. I am sure it saddens him to see how today BBC's sports output is something which would never have been tolerated in the old days.

Paul had a superb right-hand man in Ronnie Noble. He was a former newsreel cameraman who served in the war as a war correspondent. He was captured in Italy but escaped to Switzerland. At a party there he was introduced to a German officer of the old Prussian brigade, who suggested that Germany and Britain should make peace and then combine to attack Russia. Knowing Ronnie I can guess what he said to the German. Later Ronnie crossed the border into France, where he worked with the Resistance.

One other stalwart of the sports team was Fred Clarke, a sound recordist par excellence. The BBC film teams worked with a smaller crew than many others, and Fred not only made certain that the sound was 100 per cent but he was the quickest loader and unloader of a film cassette I have ever met.

Quite often we were criticized by people who didn't understand how the job was done. We would cover a football game for an edited highlights show with two film cameras. Fred Clarke would keep his eye on the counter of Camera One and when the film was running out he would say the word and the cameraman would move to Camera Two and continue shooting. Fred would cover by letting the film in Camera One run out. He would unload the camera and then with his hands in what was called a film bag, would extract the film from the case, make sure that no light got to it, and put it into a cassette. He would then see that Camera One was reloaded.

Yes, so far so good. But film cameras were temperamental things and you could stake your mortgage on one of them jamming some time during the day. If the other camera had been reloaded there was no problem. If the other camera had not been reloaded, we were caught with our trousers round our ankles. We couldn't shoot anything until the jam was unjammed and until the other camera was loaded. And it is Sod's Law that during that panic situation some unhelpful footballer would score a goal!

I remember one terrible occasion at Ninian Park, Cardiff, where Wales were playing England and England took the lead 1–0. You can almost guess the rest of the story, can't you? Wales won 2–1 with a couple of splendid goals, but what happened on both occasions? Yes, we had a camera jam!

Now no one in his right mind could blame the Welsh fans. They protested in their hundreds in telephone calls and vitriolic letters – most of which were addressed to me, the humble commentator who had nothing to do with the pictures – but, Scouts' honour, cross my heart and hope to die, I am not telling a porky. That is what actually happened and it had nothing to do with the 'English Broadcasting Corporation', as the Welsh loved to call us, wanting to ignore Wales scoring.

There were plenty of other incidents like this. Once we covered a Glasgow Old Firm game, and if you don't know what the Old Firm game is, ask a Scottish relative. For those who don't have one I can tell you it means a Celtic *v.* Rangers game or a Rangers *v.* Celtic game. (One has to be neutral on occasions like that!) We had just got telecine, a recording device which could film the picture shown by the electronic cameras. In the first half little happened and I believe the score was 0–0. So, in the Glasgow studios they broke for a cup of tea (or something) and the lens cap was put on the camera.

In the second half all hell broke loose. Players were sent off, fans fought and one of the teams (I must admit I can't remember which) won by a score you don't expect when Celtic meet Rangers (or Rangers meet Celtic). Then came the bombshell: the somebody who had put the lens cap on at half-time had forgotten to remove it for the second half so we saw absolutely two-thirds of the square root of nothing at all. Thankfully the culprit was a Scot and we left Scotland to decide whether he was a 'green' or a 'blue' (for the uninitiated, a Celtic or a Rangers fan).

These howlers were on a programme called *Sports Special*, which was the forerunner of *Match of the Day*. Another beauty was when it was decided to show a north-east 'derby' – Newcastle United *v.* Sunderland. We were full of excitement about this game and two aircraft had been chartered to fly the film to London, which was the only place in the United Kingdom where you could get it processed on a Saturday. When we viewed the film there was nothing on it – or, in professional terms, the film was fogged.

As the presenter of the programme it was my job to explain

what had gone wrong, so I just made it short and simple: 'We did hope to show you highlights of the Newcastle United *v.* Sunderland game but sadly the film was fogged.'

Once again I could understand the fans being irate, but when Members of Parliament came out with statements like, 'I was at the game and the weather was excellent. There was no fog at all,' you had to worry about the intelligence of those elected to rule us in the Mother of all Parliaments. If they didn't understand what had happened they could have asked and they would have been told. No wonder it is believed that politicians gave rise to the saying, 'The more people talk, the less they know what they are talking about.'

Nobody can be right all the time, and there was one occasion when I was assigned to cover a game between Charlton Athletic and Huddersfield Town. At the last minute Paul Fox changed his mind because he couldn't see that match being all that exciting. So I was sent to report on another game. Don't ask me which one it was because I had forgotten it by the Sunday morning. As John Macadam would have said: 'It was much ado about nothing nothing.'

When I got to the studio, Paul Fox told me the story of the Charlton *v.* Huddersfield game. It was one of those days that will be for ever etched in the history of Charlton Athletic, and to a lesser extent in that of Huddersfield Town. The match which was supposed to be of no interest turned out to be one of the most thrilling, most amazing, in fact one of the most unbelievable games in the history of the Football League.

Huddersfield Town dominated the first half, and with just twenty-three minutes to go they were leading 5–1 against a Charlton side which had been reduced to ten men by an injury to Derek Ufton, who had been taken to hospital. Ufton, as all Charlton supporters will know, was also an excellent Kent cricketer, and is now on the board of Charlton Athletic Football Club. Twenty-three minutes to go, Charlton down to ten men and trailing to five goals to one. The result was a foregone conclusion. But in football nothing is certain. Charlton made a remarkable recovery. Johnny Summers scored five goals and Charlton won the game 7–6.

What a game to miss!

Another stalwart of the sports team was a brilliant cameraman called Alan Prentice. He and Alan Clarke were a terrific double act of sound recordist and cameraman. Actually we began to pronounce Alan's name as 'Alan Prentithay' with a Spanish accent after a memorable night out in Madrid. We had finished our work and gone to a night club to enjoy some flamenco. As the night wore on, some of the customers began to talk loudly among themselves and pay little attention to the artistes, who, incidentally, were brilliant.

Suddenly Alan Prentice leapt to his feet at the end of one number, stepped on to the stage, grabbed the microphone and berated the rowdies. He told them that if they didn't want to appreciate the artistes they should leave so that other people could continue to enjoy the show. He ended his speech with, 'So shut up or get out.'

The rest of us expected a full-scale riot to develop, but Mr Prentice won the day. Not a soul left and there was quiet for the rest of the performance, at the end of which the artistes came and thanked us, or rather Alan, for what he did. Alan by this time was full of the flamenco spirit (and other spirits) and called for some wine and food for the artistes.

Our eyes boggled at the thought of the price of such generosity. When it came, the bill was astronomic, but by pooling our money we managed to cover it, and dawn came with handshakes and '*abrazos*' all around. We didn't have a peseta between us for a taxi back to the hotel. A great fellow as well as a great cameraman was our Alan Prentice.

Most of the escapades I have mentioned came after we had started the *Sports Special* programme, which, as I have said, was the prototype for the forthcoming *Match of the Day*. We began Saturday after the early evening news at 7.15 with a short programme called *Today's Sport*, consisting of the football results and a swift résumé of events. Then around ten o'clock we had *Sports Special* with film of some games and a round-up for the day's sport.

Today's Sport programme was transmitted with one fixed camera from a tiny studio, the same studio used by the news readers who preceded us. In fact, the news reader was flanked by the weather man and me and we did a quick shuffle when the camera was turned off between programmes.

Sports Special was a much more difficult kettle of fish but it had been well researched. In fact before we went on air we did two pilot programmes and everyone who had taken any part in them was asked to write a report and make suggestions for any changes. For the first pilot I had to cover Portsmouth *v.* Blackpool at Fratton Park. Paul Fox came with me and after the match we dashed by car to a nearby airfield to board a helicopter for our trip back to London. Now, at that time I was 15 stone and bulky, Paul Fox was 16 stone and bulkier, and we found it difficult to fit into the helicopter. Once we were settled in, the helicopter seemed to object to carrying such a weight and took an interminable time to get airborne. When the reports came in we found that the helicopter pilot had written a short and sweet request: 'Please could those two stout gentlemen not fly together in future.'

The first programme was a failure, but there was a big improvement for the second pilot and on Saturday, 10 September 1955, *Sports Special* went on air for the first time.

I felt very strange in the studio in Lime Grove (now a block of apartments) introducing a programme entitled *Sports Special* because my very first radio broadcast in Manchester was in a programme with that same name.

As well as commentating on a game each Saturday and my television work, I made many trips abroad to cover international matches. It was at the time of the emergence of the great Hungarian national side and Hungary were all the rage in Europe. For four years they had been undefeated. They were the Olympic Games gold medal winners from 1952. In Britain we smiled ruefully at the way these alleged amateurs could get away with it. In our eyes the Hungarians were professionals, though they said they were not. They didn't get paid for playing football, they got paid for being army officers – who never attended a parade.

In those days every country had its own ideas about what constituted an amateur and what constituted a professional. We were cynical enough to say that an amateur was someone who didn't pay income tax on the money he earned. Today there is no difference. Everybody and anybody can be a part of the Olympic Games, which still calls upon the athletes to support that hypocritical oath to amateurism while the Olympic Committee allows, for instance, professional tennis players to take part in the Games. But now that we have synchronised swimming, and perhaps in the not-too-distant future tiddly-winks in the Olympic Games does anyone care any more?

So we were willing to welcome the Hungarians to Wembley in November 1954. We had just drawn 4–4 against the Rest of Europe and we felt pretty confident.

The weekend before they came to London, Hungary played Sweden in Stockholm. The English press flocked over there to watch them and some came home to say we would have no trouble. The Hungarians could only draw with Sweden, they screamed. Only draw with Sweden? That sounded as if Sweden were a pushover when in reality they fielded a team well capable of beating England. Stan Mortensen, who led the England forward line against the Rest of Europe, was not so optimistic. 'It was not the strongest European side,' he said, 'but we were lucky to get the draw.' What happened is now history. Hungary became the first foreign side to beat England at Wembley. It was not so much a beating as a severe thrashing – 6–3.

The following spring, in 1954, just before the World Cup began in Switzerland, we played the return match in Budapest. Bedford Jezzard, the Fulham centre forward, was chosen to lead our attack and the *Daily Express* headline read, 'Jet Jezzard will Blitz Magyars'.

Hungary won 7–1 and it is difficult to recall how on earth we got one.

To the Hungarians the victory in Budapest was just another win. What mattered to them was the victory at Wembley in November 1953. It was so important that they decided in 1993 to have a big commemoration of the fortieth anniversary of their great triumph. They invited all the surviving English players to join all the surviving Hungarian players in the celebrations in Budapest. They also invited the Dutch referee, Leo Horn, and they were kind enough to invite me.

The Hungarian players who were still alive and kicking were Buzanski, Czibor, Grosics, Hidegkuti and Puskas. The only English players who could attend were Sir Stanley Matthews, George Robb and Jackie Sewell. We were all sorry the English captain, Billy Wright, couldn't make the trip. He was dying of cancer.

As hosts the Hungarians were as magnificent as they were footballers. We stayed on Margarets Island, surrounded by the River Danube, which is anything but blue as it flows through the city of Budapest, which is in fact two cities, Buda and Pest. One of the many bridges that straddle the Danube is an exact replica of London's Hammersmith Bridge. The only difference between the Hungarian version and the English is that the Hungarian replica is in proper working order whereas, it seems, London's Hammersmith Bridge will never work again.

During our stay we were presented to the President of Hungary, we were taken to pay homage at the graves of those members of the team who were no longer with us, we went to the wine country and we were fed and watered in a most magnificent manner. We even had luncheon at a restaurant which was frequented by all the heads of state and senior officials on state visits to Hungary. Nothing was too good for the English.

On the three evenings of our visit we were entertained in different ways. On the first night we were taken to a famous sports club where we met some forty or more Olympic medal winners, and were then treated to a traditional Hungarian meal – goulash soup, meat and spicy sausage and dumplings, and, of course, excellent Hungarian wine. Well, there were a lot of toasts to be drunk!

The second evening we were taken to a nightclub with a typical Hungarian orchestra – violins, cimbaloms, the lot. There was also an excellent cabaret. And, of course, the superb Hungarian wine. Well, there were a lot of toasts to be drunk!

The third and final night was the really big one – a grand banquet and cabaret broadcast by Hungarian television. The compère for the evening was Tomas Vitray, a commentator with whom I had worked often. He introduced all the players and then brought me on to the stage. In 1953 there was no television in Hungary, so it was not until a few years later that the Hungarian people were able to watch the tape with my commentary that the BBC had given them.

In 1953 the radio commentary from Wembley was given by Hungary's foremost radio commentator, George Szepesi. It was an unfamiliar experience for him to do his job from a seat in the commentary box, for Szepesi had his own technique. In Hungary he used to do his radio commentaries walking, and sometimes running, up and down the touchline.

Many people have tried to do that but few have succeeded because they have never been able to accept fully that while silence may be death on radio, it can well be golden on television. George Szepesi never took the risk of swapping from radio to television. Eventually he went on to become one of his country's representatives on FIFA, football's ruling body.

The highlight of our last evening in Budapest was the appearance of a massed choir of toddlers, youngsters, teenagers and grown-ups who sang a song written in commemoration of the Wembley victory. It was a catchy tune which I am sure was top of the Hungarian hit parade. The only people who didn't join in the singing were us English. But then we didn't know the words. I was told, though, that the song was a call for another 6–3 victory.

The Hungarians were delighted to hear how Geoffrey Green, the football correspondent of *The Times*, described that incredible Puskas goal when he dragged the ball back with the sole of his left boot, pivoted on his right foot and then fired a left-foot shot into the net. Billy Wright did come across and try to block Puskas's way to goal, but in the words of Geoffrey

Green, 'Billy Wright rushed into the tackle like a fireman racing to the wrong fire.'

An unforgettable night lingered on into an unforgettable dawn – well, there were still some more toasts to be drunk – and I got back to my hotel around four in the morning. There was just enough time to complete my packing and go by car to the airport to catch the 6 a.m. KLM flight to Amsterdam en route for London.

In London they were waiting for me to do my work on the two programmes Channel Four put out on Saturdays and Sundays on Italian football. The snag was that Amsterdam was enveloped in fog and so, too, was London so I had to kick my heels in Amsterdam airport waiting for the fog to lift.

As I sat and stared and wished for a break in the weather, I could not help but compare Hungary's celebration of a victory in one match against England with the Football Association's lack of interest in commemorating the anniversary of our winning the World Cup. Asked how the Football Association was going to celebrate the twenty-fifth anniversary of our greatest day in football, an official at Lancaster Gate said that nobody had given a moment's thought to a celebration.

So the Stars' Organization for Spastics (now known as Scope), led by Bob Wilson, decided to do the job for the FA. They held a dinner in the Banqueting Hall at Wembley and invited the whole England squad and their wives. Franz Beckenbauer was there representing West Germany. During the evening I was asked about my memories of 30 July 1966 and I said that I would like to meet once again Wolfgang Weber, who became my hero by scoring that equalizer in the ninetieth minute. The reason? Simply that if he hadn't done so England would have won 2–1, there would have been no Geoff Hurst hat-trick, nobody would have come on to the pitch, so I would never have said what I did and everyone would have forgotten me. As I finished my little piece, in walked Wolfgang Weber, immaculately dressed in the dinner jacket, and Franz Beckenbauer called out, 'Wolfgang has just walked in.' He had driven all the way from Cologne to be at the function. So we drank a few toasts!

11

My Days with Formula One

In the 1950s the market place was changing. Independent television was getting into its stride, opening the gates for commercials slotted at intervals into the programmes. Commercial radio, then confined to the pirate stations (although they deserved the title of 'pioneer' stations), was not far off being legalized.

It was then that I was invited to become a client of the Edward Sommerfield organization. This was more of a personal management group than an agency, and Teddy Sommerfield, who headed the firm, not only negotiated contracts but also advised on which offers to accept and which to reject. In short, he wanted full control.

The more you got to know Teddy the more you realized what a great worrier he was. He loved to drive to Italy in the summer, but he always insisted on packing the vehicle with food and water, obviously not trusting what the French and Italians had to offer, and, believe it or not, engine oil for his car. And he worried about his clients. Just before I left for Rome as a member of the BBC team for the 1960 Olympic Games, he said to me, 'Look after Peter West. He hasn't been abroad as much as you have, so don't let him drink too much of the wine.' The best advice was, of course, to stick to the wine.

Helping Teddy to run the organization was Stanley Barnett, a former musician who played the violin, and Sheelagh O'Donovan, an efficient Irish lass who would not be bamboozled by anyone. She dealt with the accounts, she was secretary and adviser to both Teddy and Stanley and, in short, she was simply indispensable. Care and efficiency were the two watchwords in the Sommerfield organization. Every letter was checked and double-checked, every contract was scrutinized by the company's lawyers.

I was only a beginner in this world, unlike some of the other clients. Eamonn Andrews was the star, fronting as he did the brilliant *Sports Report* on Saturdays for radio, and on television hosting *What's My Line?* and *This Is Your Life*. Peter West joined the organization just before me, and after me came Harry Carpenter.

I had, at the time, no firm contract with the BBC. I was employed purely on an ad hoc basis and whatever the BBC offered I accepted. My first commentary, for instance, earned me just £6. Now it was a different ball game. I remember sitting in Teddy Sommerfield's office in London's Golden Square one afternoon while he negotiated with someone at the BBC on my behalf. He was making the point that whenever I did a job abroad it would take me three days – one day to travel to the venue, one day to do the commentary, and one day to return to the United Kingdom. Therefore, he reasoned, in addition to my commentary fee I should be paid a fee for each day I was travelling and not able to do any other work. It seemed to me that the BBC were not agreeing too heartily to that and I could see the whole of my career collapsing before it had time to get started.

I was almost a nervous wreck and Teddy recognized this. He

told me it would take a little time to finalize the agreement, but I need have no worries. He handed me a ticket for a film première, told me to go and enjoy myself and then give him a ring at home when the show was over.

The first telephone box I saw when I left the cinema I was in it. Teddy's words will always remain with me: 'I hope you enjoyed the film and that you will also enjoy my news. I've agreed a three-year contract, the BBC have agreed to pay you for the days you spend travelling and they have also agreed that no matter by what means you travel you will travel First Class.' I could hardly believe my ears.

One of the many things I admired about Teddy Sommerfield was his insistence that both parties to an agreement honoured it. He found out once that I travelled Economy Class to Glasgow on British European Airways, as it was then called. I pointed out that the rest of the crew were on that particular flight, which left Heathrow about ten o'clock in the morning, whereas the flight with First Class accommodation took off at eight.

'Then,' said Teddy, 'you should have caught the eight o'clock flight. You are entitled to First Class travel and if the BBC find out you were willing to fly Economy they will claim you should fly Economy every time. Then they will follow up with third class rail travel and all that.'

Edward Sommerfield was a shrewd gentleman and a gentleman who was true to his word.

One battle he had to fight with the BBC was when the *Scottish Sunday Express* engaged me to be the chairman of their sports panel which travelled the length and breadth of Scotland answering questions posed by the audience. I think I was chosen because of the criticism I had made on television about Scotland's attitude to the World Cup in 1954. Not a single word would I retract even today.

Some of the Scottish FA officials claimed that my comments were rubbish, and one or two of the letter-writers accused me of being a communist. And though many huffed and puffed the majority of letters attacking me came from non-Scots, proving that the real Scots were ashamed at what happened and still hoped that Scotland could regain their reputation for decent football. Among all this I was glad to receive a message of support from Cecil McGivern, then the Controller of BBC Television Programmes. It read: 'Sincere congratulations on first-class job you are doing. Good wishes, McGivern.'

I loved travelling around with the *Scottish Sunday Express* forum, although sometimes the schedule was a bit brutal. I remember once flying from Glasgow to London, then on to Rome, for a football match, back to Glasgow, and finally to Oban by car. And the journey back from Oban to Glasgow by car in a blizzard was a frightening experience.

I met some wonderful people on my tours round Scotland. Willie Waddell, that glorious Scottish winger, was always introduced as 'the old man of the panel', so he insisted on giving his age in years, months and days. Then there was Bobbie Evans, the tenacious wing-half of Celtic and Scotland, and Jock Stein, then the captain of Celtic, who once brought the house down by saying his favourite player was fellow panellist George Young, the captain of Rangers. We also often had Willie Woodburn with us, and although he was once suspended *sine die* for misconduct by the Scottish Football Association he was nevertheless one of the finest defenders Scotland ever had.

Luck always plays a big part in anyone's career, and it was a lucky break which led me into fronting a very enjoyable, very lucrative and very popular commercial. At the time I was living in Worcester Park, Surrey and opposite my house was a hut used by the local Boy Scouts troop. Though the hut was fenced off from the road and hardly visible, one or two people raised objections mainly because of the noise the youngsters made. I was asked to join in the protest but I refused because I would rather see a hut used for teaching young lads how to be good citizens than have an army of hooligans roaming the streets. The protest didn't get anywhere, I am happy to say. I was even happier when I went to be interviewed by an advertising agency who wanted someone to front a series of commercials for Dunlop tyres. I have a feeling that I shot into pole position when one of the directors of the agency saw me. His name was Ivan Stainer and he was the chairman of the Scout Troop's Parents' Association. I got the job.

In those days Dunlop were big in Formula One motor racing. Just about every team relied on Dunlop tyres and quite a few had Dunlop disc brakes. My job was to go to every Grand Prix, interview the winning driver immediately after his lap of honour (he would, of course, have been driving on Dunlop tyres!), then fly back to Gatwick, clear customs and hop on a helicopter from Gatwick to the studios in Teddington. The commercial went out live at nine o'clock the same night.

I have to admit that I have never been a motor racing fan. It's too noisy and in those days it was difficult to follow and know who was in the lead. So, as I had nothing to do until the end of the race, I was able to wander about at will. My pass took me almost everywhere, except into one of the competing cars (and I had no desire to do that).

Once I decided to watch the race and sat in the stand next to a family, all of whom were keen fans. I then learned how you watch a Grand Prix as a team. Mum had on her knee a big lap chart, and Dad called out the numbers as they passed him. He was absolutely magnificent because the cars were not exactly idling and he never missed a number. Mum, meanwhile, had her head down as she filled in the chart. She never saw a thing. In fact, if a car had leapt the barrier and flown into the stand she would not have seen it until it landed in her lap. All the same, at the end of the race she had a complete picture from start to finish. No doubt she went home and watched a video of the race and, with the aid of her lap chart, she enjoyed it all over again. Did people have videos in those days?

Grand Prix racing was not the big business it is today. Those were the days of Stirling Moss, Jackie Stewart, Jack Brabham, Graham Hill, Mike Hawthorne and so many more. The drivers were the experts, the real stars. Rarely did you get a car that was so fast that it left the others for dead. Today it seems to be a computerized sport, whereas when I was doing the Dunlop commercials it was 100 per cent sport with the driver adding his skill to the power of his car.

Of course, the drivers were desperately keen to win, but in no way would they use what I call dodgem tactics and try to force an opponent off the track – there were rules and you stuck by them or nobody wanted to know you. One unwritten law was that every driver honoured his superiors. If you were the team's No.3 driver you would do all you could, within the rules, to make sure that your No.1 and No.2 finished in that order. It didn't happen one year when Ferrari were flavour of the season. Their three cars swept ahead at the start with the No.3 driver, of whom I had never heard and whose name still escapes me – as it probably escapes the memories even of Grand Prix aficionados – leading the field, with his two colleagues close behind. It stayed like that until the run in for the chequered flag. It was obviously going to be a Ferrari 1,2,3, but who was going to be No.1? The young unknown was supposed to move over and be happy with third place, but either he didn't understand or he was being bloody-minded. He stuck there as the leader and he took the chequered flag.

By the terms of our contract we had to interview the unknown. After all, he'd won, hadn't he? And he hadn't breached any Formula One rules. He might have broken a Ferrari rule, but we were television doing a commercial for Dunlop so that was none of our business.

I remember the day well. The heat was sweltering and the poor winner was almost out on his feet. His driver's uniform was unzipped, the ever-helpful attendants brushed his face, his neck, his chest and under his arm pits with blocks of ice. The champagne corks had been popped and the winner's manager, coach, agent, father or whatever he was, behaved like a pain in you know what. He kept complaining that the champagne he was drinking was too warm, so one of the people helping the winner to cool down dropped a lump of ice which had circumnavigated the winner's chest, arms pits and goodness knows where else into the glass of the 'too warm champagne' being drunk by the manager, coach, agent or father.

The only response we got was, 'Ah, that's better.' Every man to his taste, I say! Incidentally, that young driver never drove for Ferrari again. I am not really surprised.

There was another wonderful occasion at Nurburgring in Germany, where the weather forecast was very dodgy. We were told that it would be fine at the start, but rain would come later. But how much later? Stirling Moss's team decided the rain would come sooner rather than later and gambled by putting wet tyres on Stirling's car right from the start. These wet tyres were called 'high hysterisis' in the trade but we ignorant idiots called them the 'high hysterectomies'. If you used them in wet weather, well and good. If you used them in dry weather the rubber would peel off at an alarming rate.

Stirling's team had taken a risk and things seemed to be going well. Stirling was going well. In the lead. But the rain hadn't come. I was standing at a corner not far from the pits and as Stirling got closer and closer to the finish without any sign of rain, I and lots of others were cheering our heads off for him. The frightening thing was that we could see the rubber peeling off his tyres on the very last lap and we just prayed that our man wouldn't be forced to retire. But Stirling Moss couldn't spell the word 'retire'. He went on round the last lap of the difficult circuit, tyres shredding to almost nothing, and he won. I saw his car in the pits and I poked my finger into the tyre. My finger went right through. There wasn't another lap in those tyres, but doesn't it prove that Stirling Moss was a driver *par excellence*?

One of the loveliest events – in fact it was the first I did for the Dunlop Grand Prix commercial – was the Monaco Grand Prix. Monaco is some place, and Monte Carlo, the capital, is . . . well Monte Carlo.

The Grand Prix is programmed to coincide with the Cannes Film Festival so it is a real mixture of motor sport and super glamour. The hotel Dunlop had booked us into was the one most of the drivers used and the abundance of glamorous female talent around was simply eye-popping. Most of it spent the day scantily dressed, decorating the swimming pool. Not only that, the hotel roof was a wonderful place from which to watch the cars practising. You could appreciate the skills of the drivers as they passed the casino and had to brake right by the hotel to take a ninety degrees turn to the right. Then downhill for a short distance before a 180 degrees tight turn to the left. If you ever go to see the Monaco Grand Prix, stay at this hotel and watch the race from its roof. It doesn't cost you any more on your room rate, but if you book a seat on the promenade grandstands it costs you an arm and a leg, and you will get crushed into the bargain. And what do you see? The cars going flat out down the promenade straight until the 180 degrees turn at the end and another flat out race back down the promenade and then into the town. Watching a Grand Prix car going straight at goodness knows what speed is only slightly more thrilling than watching the paint dry . . . and a lot less thrilling than mixing with the glamorous ladies on the roof of the hotel.

The first evening we were there my wife and I went out for dinner alone and we found a gorgeous restaurant which served the most exquisite asparagus, and at a reasonable price. The rest of the party had dinner in the hotel at bank-breaking cost. After listening to our experience, the following night it was a 100 per cent turn-out for the restaurant in the town.

Perhaps the most amazing fixture of the motor sport year is the Le Mans 24-hour race. As its name implies, it lasts exactly twenty-four hours, and there are two drivers to each car. Once upon a time they had the famous Le Mans start where the drivers stood on the side of the track and ran to their vehicles on the given signals. They then had to start their cars and scramble for the best positions. It was a thrilling but dangerous sight, and after one terrible crash in which some spectators were killed, the change was made to the more usual start.

As well as being a prestigious race it is also a carnival. The crowds are vast and when you want a rest from seeing cars flash past you, you can wander into the woods where there are restaurants of various shapes and sizes, shops and all the fun of the fair. There the passion of motor sport comes second to the passion of you-know-what.

109

A car was laid on to take me to my hotel, which was well away from the area of racing. Near to Le Mans nobody sleeps because of the noise from the car engines, so it was decided to give me and the crew a good night's sleep many kilometres from the scene of the action. But when I arrived at the hotel, it was small and certainly not five star. The bed was reasonable, but the bathroom facilities were, to put it kindly, rather inconsistent. I was not a happy bunny as I went downstairs to join the rest of the crew for the evening meal. I was fuming.

What came up next, though, made up for an erratic shower and loo. Mum was slaving away in the kitchen, daughter was the serving lass and young son looked after the drinks. So did father, but he only drank not served. The meal itself was fit for a king, fit, in fact, to take over a full programme on the *Food and Drink* show. Our fancy was tickled by one or two pre-meal glasses of Pernod. Then came the wine and later the cognac, with a lesson in how to serve it. The young son-cum-barman scorned the use of an optic or any other measure. He poured the spirit from the bottle straight into the goblet. Miraculously he served just the right amount, and to prove it he gently turned the goblet on to its side and the cognac came right to the rim.

At every venue Dunlop had a huge caravan or marquee to entertain their VIP guests. At the end of the race the winner did his lap of honour, received his trophy and was then brought straight to the Dunlop caravan or marquee. It was there we made the commercial. Quite often the filming was of no interest to the guests, who, plied as they had been all afternoon with champagne, chatted away at an ever-increasing decibel rate. Our director was a stickler for discipline during a job and if the noise became too much he would roar at the top of his voice, 'I know it's nice quaffing the bubbly but we have an important job to do and we must have silence. So, QUIET, PLEASE.'

The commercial lasted or about two minutes with the driver telling me how wonderful the Dunlop tyres were and how he would never have won if he hadn't been using Dunlop disc brakes (only, of course if he had been using Dunlop disc brakes!) There was a little bit about the race itself before the punchline, 'So the German (or any other Grand Prix) has just been won by so-and-so on DUNLOP TYRES.'

Then it was a quick wrap-up, a dash to an aircraft waiting on a nearby airstrip and we were off with the precious film on the way to Gatwick, then to Teddington, where there would be a splendid party awaiting us. The buffet table was always laden with prawns, lobster, smoked salmon and other goodies, and the staff made certain that before anyone touched a thing, a plate would be loaded up for Kenneth and put on one side.

These commercials went on for quite a few years and were highly praised because of their topicality and for their placement immediately before the all-important nine o'clock news. Only one thing could prevent the Grand Prix commercial going on air. Fatal accident. It happened one year at Monza, in Italy.

Monza was a difficult Grand Prix to cover. It is some way from the city of Milan and the crowds are enormous. So I was flown in from Milan by helicopter and that would be my transport from the track to Milan airport. For the Milan–London Gatwick leg, which was going to be a race against time, a Caravelle aircraft had been chartered from Sabena, the Belgian airline.

I remember it was a hot day and all I wanted to do was sit in the shade. I was offered an untold number of glasses of champagne in the Dunlop hospitality area, but champagne and work don't go together. I must have been on the fifth or sixth glass of orange juice when the news came through. There had been a bad crash somewhere on the track. Rumours circulated that some spectators had been killed.

Then came the confirmation. A driver had crashed into the side of the track. He was dead and so, too, were some spectators. Within seconds the order was transmitted to London. There would be no Grand Prix commercial because of the fatality. The replacement would be an ordinary commercial for Dunlop tyres, one that did not mention motor racing.

12

The Battle of Berne

Enjoyable though the work for the Scottish *Sunday Express* and Dunlop was, my main source of income was the BBC Television Service. *Sports Special* was doing well and the viewers were beginning to realize that there was football beyond the English Channel. The World Cup competition had a lot to do with that.

The first time we as a nation got really interested in the World Cup was in 1954.

Hungary were the hot favourite, but the nation which triumphed was West Germany, taking part in the World Cup for the first time since the Second World War. They were unseeded in their group, along with South Korea. The two seeded nations in that group were Hungary and Spain, but Spain were surprisingly beaten in the qualifying rounds by Turkey, who took over Spain's place as a seeded nation. This was important because the two seeded nations played only against the non-seeded nations. They did not play each other.

It was, of course, a bad error by FIFA to seed the nations before the qualifying rounds were completed, and West Germany made full use of their advantage. They thrashed the seeded Turkey 4–1 in the first match and then had to face

Hungary in Basle, a city which stands on the Swiss border with both France and Germany.

On the far side of the stadium from the main stand there was a railway line and German supporters chartered a train so that they could watch the game without, apparently, paying any entrance fee. The stadium was packed almost to suffocation and when the teams were announced the German fans could not believe their ears. The Germans had selected what is these days called 'the alternative eleven'. In other words, they chose a weakened team to play against arguably the best side in the world. Their supporters replied with boos and whistles. Only five of the German side which faced Hungary in the first round played them in the final.

What the fans didn't appreciate was that the West Germans did not need to win the match. They could field a weakened team, lose to Hungary and play either the seeded Turkey or the unseeded South Korea in a play-off to decide which nation would go through to the second round. As South Korea lost their two matches 9–0 to Hungary and 7–0 to Turkey, the Germans had to replay against Turkey. It was a superb piece of tactical manoeuvring.

The Hungary *v.* West Germany game was little short of a farce with Hungary strolling to a victory by 8–3. But – and there one big, big but – Liebrich, the strong centre half of West Germany, made a rather violent tackle on Puskas, who was taken off injured. He did not reappear for the Hungarians until the day of the final, for which he did not look fit. We all believed that he had been selected simply to be presented with the World Cup as the Hungarian captain. It was not to be.

Although Hungary raced into a 2–0 lead inside eleven minutes, the West Germans, far from losing heart, hit back and by the seventeenth minute they had equalized. Six minutes from the end the Hungarian dream was shattered. West Germany scored the winning goal and the Hungarians had suffered their first defeat in four years.

It was an excellent World Cup with some brilliant football played by teams like Uruguay, Austria and, of course. West Germany and Hungary. Twenty-six games produced 140 goals, an average of 5.5 goals a game (no, please don't ask what is .5 of a goal!), and if I had to choose the game of the competitions I would have to go for Hungary's semi-final victory over Uruguay by 4–2, though the most amazing result was Austria's 7–5 win over Switzerland. England reached the second round but were beaten by Uruguay.

The saddest match came in the quarter-finals when Hungary met Brazil. There was no love lost between the two teams and politics seemed to rise above sportsmanship, with the Hungarians seen merely as communists and the Brazilians as undemocratic right-wingers. Hidegkuti scored the first goal for Hungary after just three minutes when he could almost have been sent off for indecent exposure. His shorts were ripped in a scuffle but he played on for a full minute and scored the opening goal before calling for a new pair of shorts.

Hungary scored a second goal not long afterwards and it was obvious that tension was rising. Arthur Ellis, the English referee, did his best to calm things down and after Brazil had equalized from a penalty kick the tension did ease and we saw some beautiful football from both sides.

The real trouble started with about twenty minutes of the match left. There were quite a few running fights, all behind Arthur Ellis's back, but he did spot enough to send Nilton Santos, of Brazil, and Jozsef Bozsik, of Hungary, to the dressing-room. As it turned out they were lucky to avoid what happened after the final whistle. Before the end Brazil had a second player sent off and Hungary finally won 4–2. Then all hell broke out. The Brazilian players and officials scuffled with the Swiss police, some of whom didn't seem to have been briefed as to what to do in case of trouble.

From my commentary position I saw one very elegant South American lady crack a gentleman over the head with a bottle and we heard many reports of fighting in the dressing-room area. I tried to get in there to see what was happening but the police said, 'No.' Thankfully I was spotted by a Scottish referee who had all the right passes and he got me through the lines of policemen and into Arthur Ellis's dressing-room.

It was about thirty minutes before everybody calmed down and an official went to the stand to bring Arthur's wife and two sons down into the safety of the dressing-room. As soon as they got there Arthur's lads said, 'Wasn't it smashing, Dad.'

But it wasn't just the two lads who were a bit bloodthirsty. Everyone in the United Kingdom seemed to be. I found that out when a thunderstorm over the Alps cut off the picture back home so I had to revert to a radio commentary. I explained about the storm but nobody believed me. The general opinion was that someone at the BBC had pulled the plug and killed the picture. But nobody had. It was a plain, common-or-garden thunderstorm. Mind you, I perhaps fuelled the suspicions by saying, 'I'm glad you can't see these disgraceful scenes back home.'

I soon learned my lesson. The newspapers and a shoal of letters made it abundantly clear that the viewers *did* want to see the blood and thunder and the skulduggery that went on. So much for the British being nice, quiet, gentle people who hate violence.

The 1954 World Cup will always be remembered as the first World Cup to be televised. Television had only just begun in

Switzerland and their people came to the BBC for help. I remember being invited to dinner at the Prospect of Whitby, a famous old pub in what used to be London's dockland. Cecil McGivern was the host and he had with him representatives of Swiss Television, myself and a man who was to play a big part in the success of the Swiss TV transmissions. His name was Bill Wright and he was the BBC's top cameraman, especially on football.

He was not only very talented but he was easy to get on with and – another Brownie point for this – he could speak German. Perhaps it wasn't the sort of German which would get him through O levels, let alone A levels, but at least it was German, which he had learned from the Germans in a prisoner of war camp.

Bill had served in the RAF during the war and been unlucky enough to be shot down. He was arrested when he was trying to escape in civilian clothes, and accused of being a spy. He was interrogated by the Gestapo and was still in grave danger of being shot as a spy when another member of the crew was picked up and identified Bill as a *bone fide* airman.

Bill Wright put his knowledge of German to good use while working with Swiss Television as their No.1 cameraman during the 1954 World Cup, and later on in his life he put to good use his knowledge of what it was like to be interrogated by the Gestapo. He didn't want to remain an Outside Broadcast cameraman all his life. His great desire was to be a producer. The snag was that the BBC knew what a great cameraman he was and didn't want to lose him. It was always said in television that being too good in your job could stifle your chances of promotion.

Bill was not one for giving up easily, and he put up a programme idea for consideration. It was a simple idea.

Contestants would answer questions on their chosen subject, but to give it a bit of Gestapo spice the questioner would be deadpan and aggressive. The lights would be dim, the introductory music a bit spine-chilling and contestant and questioner would sit facing each other, eyeball-to-eyeball.

You have probably already guessed the programme. Yes, it was *Mastermind* and the BBC decided to give it a trial run of about six weeks. But immediately it went on air it was a hit and there are many people today who deeply regret the BBC's decision to axe the programme after so many years of huge popularity. Sadly, Bill Wright, the mastermind behind *Mastermind*, did not live long enough to see his programme become one of the all-time greats, for he died some years ago.

Every World Cup has thrown up some controversy. The 1958 competition, which had its final stages in Sweden, produced a controversy which should prove to our former Minister of Sport, Mr Tony Banks, that he is way behind the times.

Some countries started to question why the United Kingdom could use its own international tournament as a World Cup qualifying group. It was unfair, they argued, because it made certain that two United Kingdom countries would reach the final stages. 'Play as one country or play as four countries and take your chance like the rest of us,' was the demand. The argument in favour of a Great Britain team is flawed, though. There is no Great Britain Football Association and there is less chance than ever of there ever being one now that Scotland and Wales have some form of home rule.

So in 1958 the four home associations said they were quite happy to be split up in the qualifying competition, and it was a shock to the rest of the world that all four – England, Northern Ireland, Scotland and Wales – qualified.

Right: My dad who began it all.

Below: With a Danish paratrooper just a few days after the liberation.

Interviewing Pelé at the Maracana stadium in Rio de Janeiro.

Receiving the Baird Silver Medal for services to television from James Logie Baird's widow Margaret.

Above: *Joan and me with Franklin Engleman and his wife at the Baird Silver Medals award ceremony.*

Below: *We had quite a party when Billy Butlin invited my late wife Joan and me to his luxurious home.*

BBC1   Sunday *tv*

Duel in the sun-the World Cup Final

1966 . . . World Cup Final – the goal that really nailed it. Hurst, chased by a German defender, lets go with a shot which rockets under the bar – it's all over! 1970 . . . World Cup Final – join David Coleman in the great bowl of the Aztec Stadium for football's greatest drama: 6.0

ENGLAND   WEST GERMANY 2

5.50 pm   *Colour*
The News
Weatherman GRAHAM PARKER

6.0   *Colour*
**World Cup
Grandstand:
The 1970
World Cup Final**
Introduced by **David Coleman**
from Mexico

The whole of the world's greatest
football occasion as it happens in
the Aztec Stadium, Mexico City

6.0
David Coleman sets the scene in
the Aztec Stadium as the crowd
of over 100,000 gathers for the
world's most important football
occasion

6.10
All the latest news from Mexico,
with comment and analysis by
the *Grandstand* team of experts,
including
JOE MERCER and DON REVIE

6.20
Meet The Finalists
Action highlights of the two
countries' progress to the World
Cup Final, and special features
introducing some of tonight's
outstanding personalities

6.50
The World Cup Final
The whole match, as it happens,
in the Aztec Stadium
With action replay of the game's
outstanding moments and expert
analysis by David Coleman and
the *Grandstand* team
Production team in Mexico
SAM LEITCH, JACK OATEN
ALEC WEEKS
Production team in London
ALAN HART, BRIAN VENNER
and FRED VINER
Executive producers
BRYAN COWGILL and ALAN CHIVERS

9.15   *Colour*
The News
with
ROBERT DOUGALL
and Weather

9.25   *Colour*
**The Sunday Film presents
A Kenneth More Season**
**The Sheriff of
Fractured Jaw**
starring
Kenneth More
Jayne Mansfield, with
Robert Morley
More, Mansfield, and Spanish loca-
tions blend in a hilarious tale of
the west – with More as a non-
violent English gunsmith who
accidentally becomes the most
feared sheriff west of Tombstone.
Many Hollywood veterans – including director Raoul Walsh –
give the film a surprisingly au-
thentic flavour.

Jonathan Tibbs......KENNETH MORE
Kate..................JAYNE MANSFIELD
Uncle Lucius.......ROBERT MORLEY
Toynbee..............RONALD SQUIRE
Masters....................HENRY HULL
Keene............WILLIAM CAMPBELL
Jack.........................BRUCE CABOT

Screenplay by ARTHUR DALES
based on a short story by JACOB HAY
Produced by DANIEL M. ANGEL
Directed by RAOUL WALSH
(Jenkinson's Guide: page 12)

11.5
Neither Hot nor Cold
Bishop **Trevor Huddleston** talks
to ROBERT KEE about the state of
the Church of England today.
Produced by SHIRLEY DU BOULAY

11.25   *Colour*
**My World . . .
and Welcome To It**
A series based on a selection of
James Thurber's famous stories
and cartoons
starring
William Windom as John Monroe
Joan Hotchkis as his wife Ellen
Lisa Gerritsen
as his daughter Lydia
Man Against the World
John Monroe recreates a slice of
American history for his daugh-
ter's homework – and starts a
most un-Civil War!
(first shown on BBC2)

11.50   *Colour*
Weatherman
Closedown

RADIO TIMES DATED 18 JUNE 1970.

The infamous billing in the Radio Times of June 1970. It showed the BBC were prepared to ignore my contract and install David Coleman in the commentator's seat for the 1970 World Cup final.

Above: *With Henry Cooper, Prime Minister Harold Wilson, and Douglas Bader, a wartime fighter-ace despite having two artificial legs.*

Right, top: *With a very young Nick Faldo.*
Right, bottom: *With H R H the Duke of Edinburgh, who later presented me with a Variety Club of Great Britain special award for services to sport.*

Below: *Never a dull moment with Gordon Banks and Nobby Stiles (or Norbert as he was christened and as Sir Alf Ramsey always called him).*

Above: *A chat with Mark Phillips and two very young future England footballers, Alan Ball and Ray Wilkins.*

Right: *Mike Tyson looks friendly enough outside the ring.*

Below: *With the great Seve Ballesteros after his runaway win in the Martini Golf Tournament at the Royal Automobile Club, Epsom in my year of captaincy.*

Above: Handing the Sportsman of the Year trophy to Ieuan Evans, the Llanelli and Wales winger.

Below: With Pierluigi Casiraghi, the Italian international before his transfer to Chelsea from Lazio, and Josephine O'Toole, an avid Lazio fan.

Maybe I am biased but I gave referee Eddie Wolstenholme (no relation) 10 out of 10 when I saw him at an Exeter City game.

Above: *Tomas Vitray, the top Hungarian TV commentator interviewing George Szepesi (another famous Hungarian commentator) and me at the banquet to celebrate the 40th anniversary of Hungary's 6-3 victory over England at Wembley in 1953.*

Right: *Not even the rain can wipe the smile off Jimmy Hill's face.*

Below: *Making a point to Ferene Puskas in Budapest. Neither Phil Rostron (then Sports Editor of the Daily Star) nor Sir Stanley Matthews seem convinced.*

The family: from left to right, daughter Lena, grandson David, son-in-law Nicholas and grand-
daughter Amy. Sadly, my eldest grand-daughter, Sarah was away on the day of the
photo session. *(Copyright: Herald Express, Torquay)*

Right: With my eldest grand-daughter Sarah.

Below: Enjoying a drink with John Charles, the best all-round footballer I have ever seen, in the Leeds pub of Peter Lorimer, another great Leeds United player.

Just before teeing off in the 1999 Golf Tournament in aid of The Welsh Rugby Union at the Bryn Meadows Golf Club.

Scotland went home early, winning just one point from their three games. England drew each one of their three qualifying games and had to face a play-off with the Soviet Union. At a press conference before the match, Walter Winterbottom, the England team manager, reminded the media that 'We haven't lost a game yet.' Geoffrey Green, that wonderful writer on *The Times*, a man who was a true romantic, replied, 'That's true, my old commander, but what is more important, we haven't won one either.'

And we didn't. The Soviet Union beat us in the play-off 1–0.

The Swedes were suspicious of the Irish team. Sweden is a strong Protestant country and one newspaper even wrote that the Irish players would be playing for their religion. The truth was that there was only one Roman Catholic in the Northern Ireland party and to prove it the whole squad went to the local Protestant church the Sunday after the newspaper story. They were then promoted to being one of the most popular teams.

Northern Ireland did magnificently. Although riddled with injuries they beat Czechoslovakia, drew with West Germany and lost only to Argentina. That put them into a play-off with Czechoslovakia, which they won 2–1 in extra time against all the odds. That victory meant they had to meet the strong French side in Norrköpping and an administrative blunder let down the players. Instead of making the long journey in a comfortable train they travelled by coach. Their tired players lost to the free-scoring French 4–0.

Wales were real heroes. They drew all their first-round games – against Hungary, Mexico and the host nation Sweden – and then beat Hungary in a play-off. This gave them a quarter-final game against Brazil and the doubtful pleasure of facing the great Pelé in his first game in the World Cup finals.

Seventeen-year-old Pelé went on to win the final against

119

Sweden against all expectations according to the Swedish manager, who said, 'If it rains and we score first we will win.' It rained, Sweden scored first and Brazil won 5–2.

Chile in 1962 showed us how to stop fans being overcharged at World Cups. The government announced that any hotels, restaurants or places of entertainment found to be overcharging would be closed immediately. There was one highly popular restaurant to which some Colombian supporters called the police. The bill had been tampered with and, true to their word, the police shut the restaurant there and then.

There was one lovely story about this competition that showed how low the players were in the opinion of the administrators. During a not-very-friendly semi-final between Chile and Brazil, a Chilean was sent off along with Garrincha, the famous Brazilian right-winger.

Usually in World Cups, players who are sent off are dealt with quickly and the minimum suspension is one match. We all wondered whether this would mean Garrincha would miss the final. A number of us were discussing this over a drink so I decided to telephone Sir Stanley Rous, at that time the President of FIFA. Sir Stanley told me, 'The Disciplinary Committee met this morning and it was decided that the Chile player should be suspended for one match and the Brazilian No.7 would be cautioned as to his future behaviour.'

How a world-famous player like Garrincha could be referred to as 'the Brazilian No.7' was beyond me. It smacked so much of the Jockey Club who would address a jockey of the status of Lester Piggott as just plain 'Piggott'.

Anyway, Garrincha played in the final, which Brazil won 3–1 after once again conceding the first goal, scored by that wonderful player, Josef Masopust. Pelé, sad to say, was discovering the price of fame. He was injured in the first match, against Mexico, and took no further part in the competition. For him it was just a foretaste of what was to come in England four years later.

One had to admire Chile for putting on the World Cup at all because the country had suffered severe earthquakes on the run-in to the competition. We were glad they had managed to put all that behind them because when we left we all felt happier for having been there. Most of us, for instance, had never seen anything like the gauchos riding their horses down the streets of sleepy old Rancagua, which nestles in the foothills of the Andes and was unfortunate enough to host the most boring game of football I have ever seen . . . England 0 – Bulgaria 0. And both sides were lucky to get nil!

No one likes to dwell on football games as grim as that England *v.* Bulgaria game because there were so many fine memories of Chile. The celebrations when the Chilean team beat the Russians were like London on VE night. Then there were the stirring stories about Bernardo O'Higgins, the revolutionary who became Chile's first president and who is revered as a national hero.

Then there was the old port of Viño del Mar, which had obviously seen better days, and the flight over the towering peaks of the Andes, breathtaking even to a hardened old aviator like myself. And nobody could miss the figure of Christ on this imposing mountain range. As they say in those parts, if Brazil can have the Cristo, so can we. And why not?

13

Writ for a Million Dollars

Though overseas trips were the icing on the cake, covering domestic football was highly entertaining and thrilling. When we went to report a league or cup game for *Sports Special* or, later, *Match of the Day*, which began in 1964, most of the clubs were very friendly, though no way would they be bossed about as they are today. Now the clubs are told when to play, what time to kick off and, I am almost certain, what colours to wear. In those good old, bad old days if we suggested the slightest change of strip we would be met by stony stares.

Nowadays teams have home colours and away colours. Some wag, probably a Manchester City fan, has suggested that Manchester United have a different strip for every day of the week. But, in the days of non-colour television – it wasn't black and white, was it, more grey and grey – if we had the temerity to suggest that one team changed the colour of their socks we would be refused point blank.

I can see their point. The fans loved their team colours, they didn't want to see their heroes playing in different coloured shirts every week. The only time a club would change their colours was if there was a clash, such as when Manchester United went to Liverpool and had to change their red shirts because Liverpool, too, played in red. Today clubs never play in the same shirts home and away.

And why? Simply because those hardy supporters who go to away games will buy both the home and away kit, and that is big business. Every change in football these days is motivated by money. Clubs can't live on their gate receipts and continue to pay the huge transfer fees and the unbelievably high wages of today's players, so they call on the commercial department to work overtime and make more and more money.

Goalkeepers, perhaps the most protected species in modern football, refused to be left behind in the fashion stakes. In the old days they wore yellow sweaters for international matches, but for ordinary club games it was a green sweater, with the occasional blue or red. Now they wear the gaudiest jerseys the kit manufacturers can design. I call them pretty frocks.

Referees and linesmen – or referee's assistants if you want to be politically correct, though few people do – no longer wear the dark shorts and dark blazer that was good enough for the likes of J. T. Howcroft, Tiny Wharton, Arthur Ellis and the rest. In the Premiership they wear coloured shirts, in the Nationwide League they wear dark shirts with wiggly lines all over them. They call it progress!

The BBC were always striving for progress. Take that great day when British athletes did the 'impossible' and broke the four-minute mile barrier. Nobody in the country knew that Chris Brasher, Chris Chataway and Roger Bannister were going to try and write yet another triumph in the record books. BBC Television, however, got wind of it and had a camera team on the spot. That very evening the country could see Roger Bannister not only completing his mile run in under four minutes but also talking about it on *Sportsview*. Yes, the BBC got him from Oxford and into the Lime Green studios in Shepherds Bush. That was BBC enterprise in those days – always alert, aiming to provide the most comprehensive coverage of sporting events possible. Sometimes this caused problems.

I remember the time when the BBC applied for a visa to enable me to cover a game between Hungary and Scotland in Budapest. When the visa didn't arrive by the time I was due to leave, Peter Dimmock, the head of Outside Broadcasts, said, 'Just go and you'll be all right. They'll issue you with a visa when you get there.'

I was reassured by the fact that my very good friend Geoffrey Green, of *The Times*, was also visa-less.

When we landed in Budapest, soldiers, armed to the teeth, came on board the aircraft to collect all passports and check visas. They quizzed Geoffrey first and in his true bohemian style he said in a loud voice, 'My old friend, I bring greetings from the working people of Britain to our great friends, the working people of Hungary. Why do I have to have a visa to greet your wonderful people?' Those were the days of the Cold War when there seemed to be little if any love between the East and the West, and I thought that was a speech good enough to get us both flung into the nearest prison, but after a lot of hassle we were given entry visas. Getting exit visas was more difficult because all the senior officials had gone to the countryside for their weekend breaks.

Some time afterwards I returned to Budapest, and again my visa didn't arrive on time. But Peter Dimmock was ever the optimist, 'You got away with it last time so you'll be all right this time.' I wasn't. Here, let me explain that in those days we didn't travel in teams. I was on my own.

I was led into a room at the airport and the door was locked with a fully armed soldier on guard outside. It was a comfortable enough room with a number of magazines on a table, not that I could read them, though I could, at least, look at the pictures. There was also a telephone. When I picked it up it worked, and knowing full well that the line was tapped, I dialled the number of the British Embassy and asked for the Press Attaché whom I knew.

It was a relief to hear his voice. 'Kenneth, you here for the match against Yugoslavia? That's great. Where are you, the Gellert Hotel?'

'No,' I replied. 'I'm locked in a room at the airport. Come and get me out.'

He guessed right first time. 'Oh, God! Not without a visa again. Stay there, I'll be right over.'

Stay there. That was rich! There was nothing else I could do. Anyway, diplomacy worked and I was taken before an official who explained that I was being released into the care of the Attaché and the nice lady from Hungarian television. I was told that she would pick me up at seven o'clock the following morning and we had to be at the Foreign Office by half-past seven. We duly arrived dead on time, and were ushered into a room when an official of the Foreign Office was sitting at a plain desk with a pile of papers in front of him.

He ignored me as if I was of no importance whatsoever and he and the television lady began talking in Hungarian. To while away the time I looked around the room and saw nothing but four bare white walls. Not a picture, not a calendar. Just nothing.

I have no idea how long the dialogue between the Foreign Office man and the television lady went on but it seemed like hours, and the Foreign Office man hadn't even given me a glance.

Suddenly he looked me straight in the face and spoke, 'So,

Mr Wolstenholme,' he said in flawless English. 'Why have you come to Budapest without a visa? For the second time?'

I tried my best to explain that we had applied for a visa but it hadn't come through and that the BBC had already announced that they would show the whole of the Hungary *v.* Yugoslavia game on the Sunday afternoon and the British people would be very disappointed if anything happened to stop the trans-mission.

He did not accept that as a reasonable explanation but said that this time I would be forgiven. But if I ever did it again, 'as soon as you get off the aircraft you will be put on to the next aircraft which is flying to a destination outside Hungary'.

As a final humiliation he made me walk down the street with the television lady to buy the required number of stamps to put on the visa. When I had done that he handed me my passport (I was glad to get that back!), smiled broadly and said, 'Now, Mr Wolstenholme, how do you think the game will go this afternoon?'

I was flabbergasted. I said something about it being a tight match, that Hungary usually did well against Yugoslavia and that the audience at home would be on Hungary's side because they had such marvellous memories of the Hungarian wonder team of Puskas and company.

Another friendly smile and he closed the meeting by saying, 'Mr Wolstenholme, you talk like a diplomat.' I hadn't the faintest idea whether he meant that as a compliment or whether it was a bit of sarcasm. I still haven't. But I do know that the Hungarian Embassy in London told me always to apply direct to them when I wanted a visa in future and not to a travel agency. This advice I took and they treated me most handsomely during the short time I had to wait for the visa to be processed. Mind you, coffee and baracs early in the morning calls for a strong constitution. But it takes some beating.

I always enjoyed visits to Yugoslavia and remember one particular occasion going to Zagreb for a Sunday international. I had to catch a Saturday evening flight because I had been working all day and then, instead of landing in Zagreb, we were diverted to Belgrade because of fog. We were offered hotel accommodation in the capital and were told we would be flown to Zagreb in the morning. I said I would rather catch a train because the fog might be slow to clear and I had a briefing at ten o'clock in the morning.

When we found out there was a train just after midnight two other fellows said they would join me. One was a Brit, the other a Norwegian, and we were all handed first-class tickets to Zagreb. They meant nothing. The train was packed with Greek workers on their way to work in Germany and all we could do was squeeze in a third-class compartment. Every Greek carried his worldly goods in a bundle and there was no hope of any comfort from the straight-backed wooden bench seats.

The Norwegian had bought some cheese from somewhere and a small bottle of slivovits and it was decided we should share this between us and then take turns to have a nap while the other two remained awake and watchful. Eventually we reached Zagreb (and the fog hadn't completely dispersed) and I just had time to get to my hotel, have a quick shave and shower, rush to the briefing meeting and then straight to the stadium.

One particular trip to the American continent during the closed season of 1959 remains vividly in my mind because a very young Jimmy Greaves was making his first tour with the England team. We were to play Brazil in Rio de Janeiro, Peru in Lima, Mexico in Mexico City and finally the United States in Los Angeles. One evening in Mexico City Jimmy was sitting in the lobby of the hotel looking pretty lonely. Three of us were going out to dinner so we asked Jimmy to join us. He was delighted to do so.

We went to a restaurant called the Catacombs where, we found out, anything could happen. Jimmy was studying the menu when a waiter walked behind him and dangled a fake spider right in front of his face. England's newest footballing star almost jumped out of his skin.

However, we persuaded him to join a short tour of the catacombs, where 'a learned professor' gave a brief lecture on Mexico's rather brutal past. There were models of men lying in their coffins and the agony on their faces showed that they had been brutally tortured. The audience, including Jimmy, listened intently until there was an ear-shattering scream and one of the 'corpses' leapt out of his coffin. If you thought Jimmy Greaves was quick off the mark on the football field you should have seen him move that night at the catacombs!

Sadly the tour was not a successful one. We lost in Rio de Janeiro, we lost in Lima and we lost in Mexico City. When we arrived at our final destination, Los Angeles, we were subjected to the usual United States immigration procedure. One of the first in the queue was Joe Mears, who was then chairman of Chelsea and also of the Football Association. When he was asked the inevitable question, 'What is the purpose of your visit to the United States?' Joe replied, 'I am the chairman of the English Football Association.'

The immigration officer looked blank and his reply brought howls of laughter, especially from the gentlemen of the media. 'English Football Association,' said the officer. 'I didn't know you limeys played football.'

And people still think that association football will become a major sport in the United States of America.

The problem for the immigration officers was the number of East European visas in the passports of the journalists and television people. Remember it was the time of the Cold War and Americans were very suspicious of any hint of communist sympathies. We had to go through long explanations that the communist countries played our game of football. I don't suppose it helped that some of us emphasized that our football was a world game not an exclusively American one, but finally we got through and set off to enjoy our stay in Los Angeles.

We saw the sights, went to all the right places and were the recipients of super hospitality. When we arrived at the venue for the game we were amused to see it was to be played on a baseball pitch. This meant that there was a huge bare patch at one end which made football a little difficult. Life was more than a little difficult when the American team scored first and things got worse when they seemed to have scored a second. The ball looked to have crossed the English line, but a friendly referee ruled otherwise and England settled down and went on to score eight goals and make it an easy (and welcome) victory.

The American sports writers and broadcasters organized a special luncheon for the visiting press and television people. Everybody who was anybody was there. As we were leaving I was approached by a gentleman who asked me, 'Are you Kenneth Wolstenholme of the BBC Television?' I told him I was and he said, 'I have to give this to you.'

He handed me an envelope and I honestly thought it was a gift. I started to open the envelope as my 'kind benefactor' quickly disappeared. I realized why when I saw he had given me a writ for $1 million against the BBC. As he had left I had no chance to tell him I had no authority to accept such documents because I was not on the BBC staff.

The Americans were furious and told me to tear up the writ and throw the pieces away, but I felt even less entitled to do that than to accept the document in the first place. It claimed that the BBC had shown a programme starring an American comedian who had signed an exclusive contract with Independent Television. I sent a cable to the BBC telling them of the writ and pointing out that I was leaving the next day for New York, where I was having a holiday. Back came the reply asking me to take the writ to the BBC office in New York. I could not help thinking that, since I was on holiday, someone from the BBC should come to my hotel to pick up the document. But life is never like that, is it?

With me at the time of this incident was Jack Wood, a sports writer on the *Daily Mail*. Never the sort of reporter to miss a story, Jack wrote a beauty for his newspaper and it made the front page. A neighbour of my mother's saw the story and hurried round to show it to my mother. The headline read, 'BBC Commentator Handed Writ For Million Dollars,' and it took her some time to realize that the BBC was being sued not me.

I never heard another word about the case, so I imagine that like so many of the writs that fly around in America this one never made the courts.

Jack Wood and I had a great time in Lima during that tour. We were having a quiet drink in our hotel bar when a wedding party arrived for the reception. Jack and I were both attracted to the bride, who was an absolute stunner, and before we knew what had happened we had both been invited to join the wedding party. It transpired that the bride was the daughter of the mayor of one of Lima's suburbs, and he generously invited us to the town hall the following day for a friendly drink. Sadly, the bride had gone away on her honeymoon.

For some years Jack Wood was the golf writer for the *Mail* and he was well known for turning up at the course around midday to ferret out a likely story. Coming upon the great Gene Sarazen, from the United States, playing in a tournament, Jack interviewed him.

The following day when Jack arrived at the course he was told by all his fellow writers to 'Keep well away from Gene Sarazen.' But Jack couldn't understand what was wrong. In fact he thought the piece he telephoned to the newspaper was an excellent one. He had dictated over the telephone, 'Gene Sarazen, the sweet swinging star of yesteryear.' Sadly that is not what the copy-taker typed nor what the *Daily Mail* printed. They started the story, 'Gene Sarazen, the street singing star of yesteryear.'

No wonder Mr Sarazen was not amused.

After Celtic won the European Cup in 1967 they were called upon to play Racing Club of Argentina for what was called the World Club Championship. The first leg was a bruising contest in Glasgow which Celtic won 1–0. But Jock Stein, the Celtic manager, was furious that the game wasn't televised. The reason it wasn't on television was that the Football League would not allow it because there were League Cup ties that evening. Television could not show any games without the permission of the home association. Things are different today because different TV companies have bought the rights to certain games, but that was not allowed in the old days.

Celtic took that slender lead to Argentina, and they had another bruising contest before losing 2–1. In those days there were no penalty shoot-outs or extra time with the golden goal, so Celtic and Racing Club had to replay. There was something else missing in those days. The away goals rule whereby goals scored away from home count double in the event of the scores being level after extra time. If the away goals rule had been in force at the time, Celtic would have won the trophy because the scores were level at two goals each, but Celtic had scored one away from home; Racing Club hadn't.

The replay in Montevideo was a football match from hell. The BBC was not allowed to cover it live but the powers-that-be decided to record the action and put on a commentary later. It was the sort of game in which it is a miracle every player got out alive. I was called in to do the commentary with orders to pinpoint incidents which were about to happen. This annoyed the Scots because they thought that it was a way to put the blame on Celtic, which it didn't, and Jock Stein vigorously attacked the BBC, and me especially, although when the edited highlights were shown he was in an aircraft coming back from the South Atlantic.

What Jock and many other Scots did not realize was that the BBC could not show the game as it happened, so the only way a commentary could be put on the highlights was to have a scripted one with the commentator reading the script. But I suppose we cannot expect everyone to understand the complexities of television. Even people who work in it find it difficult, especially in these modern times when the television world has become so complicated.

Mind you, the Scots have always been suspicious of anybody who is not Scottish, especially in football. When Celtic won the European Cup in 1967 I described them as being the first British team to do so, which was correct. But the Scots objected because I didn't say they were the first Scottish team to win the competition. To my mind if you become the first British person to do something it means you have succeeded where all other Brits (in Celtic's case England, Northern Ireland and Wales) had failed. And I know full well that if I had described Celtic as the first Scottish team to win the European Cup, every Scot would have objected and reminded me that they were the first *British* club to do so. You just can't win!

Incidentally, Celtic did not win the cup in the Stadium of Light, the home of Benfica in Lisbon, as some of our newspapers told us in the build-up to the 1999 final. They won it in the National Stadium, a few miles away in Estoril.

In 1968, after Manchester United won the European Cup, it was their turn. They had to face Estudiantes de la Plata in the World Cup Championship. The first leg was to be played away, so we all headed for Buenos Aires, where we were treated magnificently.

The big event was a polo match followed by a typical Argentine barbecue. Now Argentines excel at polo and we discovered that we were watching nine handicap players, which is equivalent to scratch at golf. Perhaps none of us could really follow the game but we certainly all enjoyed the barbecue. In Argentina they love their meat and we were plied with steaks, chops, sausages and black pudding – the players watched their diet carefully – and at a reception later we were presented with beautiful wallets of the best leather.

One man had been designated to look after us media chaps. He was extremely helpful and gave each of us his card, asking us to ring him at any time of the day or night if we had any problems.

He was an excellent polo and rugby player, but with a bit of a chequered career. On one occasion he was carried off unconscious in a rugby match. When he signalled he was ready to come back the referee sent him off for being one of the instigators of the fracas which had led to his being knocked unconscious. He was serving a life suspension from rugby so he concentrated on his polo. A tough lot of *hombres* are the Argentines!

On the day of the match I got to the Boca Juniors stadium, the venue of the game, a fearsome arena with huge stands rearing at an angle from the touchline, very early because we wanted to film inside the United dressing-room. The officials would not let us in. Only players, club and match officials and FIFA representatives were allowed into the dressing-rooms. Even the fact that we had a contract with United cut no ice. Were we pleased to see Matt Busby and his team arrive! He immediately gave us permission to set up our cameras and we were able to record all – or, nearly all – that went on in the dressing-room before a big game.

When the match kicked off in a ground packed to suffocation but where the only Man U fans were the British folk who lived and worked in Buenos Aires, United's game plan was obviously to get Nobby Stiles to burst down the middle whenever he could. This he did splendidly only to be met by some more than tough tackling and at times some very dubious offside decisions.

The newspapers had carried lots of stories about Nobby, mentioning the fact that he wore contact lenses while he was playing, and that if one of them were dislodged, Nobby was as good as blind. The Estudiantes defenders succeeded in knocking one of Nobby's lenses out and we were subjected to a comic scene with Nobby Stiles on his hands and knees searching for his contact lens on the grass. Anyone with 20/20 eyesight would have had the greatest difficulty finding a contact lens on a huge football field; Nobby Stiles had no chance.

Then the inevitable happened. Nobby burst down the middle for the umpteenth time and had a great chance to score before a linesman raised his flag and the referee once more blew for offside. Nobby raised his right arm in disbelief and was promptly sent off.

As he made the long, lonely walk round the outside of the pitch he held his head up high, his face wreathed in the well-known Nobby Stiles smile and his jaunty walk seemed to scream out, 'I'm Nobby Stiles.' He was pelted with anything the home fans could find but they couldn't knock Nobby out of his stride or wipe out his car-to-ear grin.

The following day I interviewed Nobby, who had been downtown shopping. He told me how people had applauded him and gone up to him to shake his hand. Yes, even the Argentines were captivated by this tremendous little fellow from Manchester. It was reminiscent of what happened in London the day after Antonio Rattin, the Argentine captain, had been sent off in the 1966 World Cup tie against England. Just as Stiles was fêted in Buenos Aires, Rattin was fêted in London.

United had lost 1–0 in Buenos Aires, and it was now time to head for home. But there was bad news from the flight deck as we prepared to leave. One of the engines had a fault so we would be delayed until it was rectified. No one likes to hear that their aircraft has developed a fault and Manchester United people like it less than most, for obvious reasons. Brian Kidd was especially nervous but I tried to reassure him that it was far better that they discovered the fault while we were still on the ground than when we were in the air.

He agreed and eventually the flight home went off without a hitch.

Then came the second leg, which was not the happiest of matches and ended 1–1, a score which gave the South

Americans the victory on aggregate of goals from the two games. As the players were leaving the field at the end of the game, one of the United lads seemed to retaliate when provoked by one of the Argentines. This was shown on the edited highlights of the game later that evening and the United chairman, Louis Edwards, father of the present chairman, Martin Edwards, was fuming. He accused me of showing the incident to bring his club into disrepute.

All the explanations in the world that commentators have no control over the editing of any programme were of no avail, and it was Sir Matt Busby who was the peacemaker. He said to me, 'Come into my office, Kenneth, and have a drink. Directors don't understand those things.'

14

1966 and All That

The 1950s had been exciting. To be part of the development of television was a great thrill, and I felt very proud when I was awarded the Baird Silver Medal for Services to Television, especially as only twelve were awarded and they were presented by the widow of Logie Baird, the gentleman who invented the medium which has informed us, entertained us, excited us, thrilled us, horrified us and sometimes made us hopping mad.

I didn't think the 1960s could beat the 1950s, but I was wrong because in the 1960s there were many strides forward. Unfortunately, as far as I was concerned, there was also more than a little sadness. I could not easily forget the six times our house was burgled. I once felt I should do what the late Tommy Trinder did when he had uninvited guests. He put a sign outside his house which read: 'To intending burglars: Don't break in. You are too late. Everything's been nicked.'

Always after a burglary the police made frequent visits to assure us that they were continuing with their inquiries. One evening the doorbell rang and I opened the door to see a young policeman standing there. I said to him, 'Good evening, officer. Nice to see you and I know you are doing your best to catch the villains.'

Without a smile on his face and in a very official voice he asked, 'Are you Kenneth Wolstenholme?' When I agreed I was, he handed me a piece of paper and told me it was a summons for illegal parking. I felt like killing him! I discovered later that it was his first day on duty at the local police station. He was straight out of training, so when the summons came through it was decided he was the man to deliver it. Not a word was said to him about the number of burglaries I had suffered, including one only a few days previously. Coppers can be cruel to their young recruits sometimes, can't they?

I remember on another occasion I overstayed my welcome on a parking space. It was in the City of London and I gasped when I saw the signature on the ticket . . . PC Goring. It wasn't the ticket so much as the signature. Fancy being booked by a policeman with the name of Goring!

A few weeks later I spoke at a dinner given by the City of London Fraud Squad (sometimes called the most overworked police force in the world) and I mentioned my horror at being booked by a PC Goring. Afterwards I was invited to have a drink in the canteen of a nearby police station and would you believe it, it was the one at which PC Goring was stationed. Not only that but as we walked in my hosts saw PC Goring. They called him over and insisted he bought me a drink and he saw the funny side of it. He assured me he was no relation of the infamous Hermann and he even apologized for booking me.

But forget my traffic offences – they have not been all that numerous – because there was a much more bitter blow to me in the 1960s. Our daughter, Elisabeth, who was fourteen, seemed unwell. She was pale and listless whereas she was usually happy and full of beans. We were worried so my wife decided to take her to the doctor.

I got home about seven o'clock that evening and found a note on the kitchen table. Elisabeth was in hospital. My wife had been taken to the local pub by two friendly neighbours, who didn't think it fair or wise for my wife to be on her own.

As I walked into the Glyn Arms (as the pub was then called) near East Ewell station, I was met by the owner, Ray Duval, a great friend of mine. He gave me a large Scotch and told me to sit down. 'You are going to need both,' were his ominous words. Then my wife came to tell me the news that Elisabeth had acute myloblastic leukaemia and would be dead inside six months.

Once I had recovered from the shock I tried to think of who might be able to help. My first thought was the great surgeon Dickson Wright, but I didn't have his telephone number with me. Then I thought of Billy Butlin, who was entertaining guests at the National Sporting Club in London's Café Royal. I rang there but was told it was a rule that members could not be disturbed during dinner unless it was a matter of life or death. I told them it was.

When Billy Butlin came to the telephone I told him the story and he said, 'Stay where you are and I will find Dickson Wright and ask him to telephone you.' In no time at all, Dickson Wright, whom I knew, was on the phone telling me that he was a surgeon and leukaemia was not a surgical illness. But he promised to get hold of Dr Bodley Scott – and he did.

I gave the doctor the rough outline of the situation and he said he would contact the hospital and make arrangements to see Elisabeth. Dr Bodley Scott was a doctor to the royal household so when he arrived at Epsom General Hospital it was like a royal visit with all the top brass present.

After examining Elisabeth he asked me what I had been told. I told him about the six months verdict and his reply was shattering: 'I think that is an optimistic forecast.' So that was it.

Not a life sentence but a death sentence because there was nothing in those days that could be done for acute myloblastic leukaemia.

The next four months were the worst of our lives. Elisabeth had wonderful care in the hospital, but it was a life of blood transfusions and cortisone injections. Sometimes she would be allowed home and she would go to school, oblivious, so we were told, of how seriously ill she was. Each time she had to go back to hospital teachers from her school – Roseberry Grammar School, which was almost opposite Epsom Hospital – would visit her and give her school work to do.

Everybody was magnificent, trying to help but not giving Elisabeth any hint of the real truth. In fact, a photographer called at our house one day and asked my wife if we would like a photograph taken of Elisabeth. He didn't have a clue about Elisabeth's condition. He was just a professional photographer wanting to drum up trade by taking pictures of children. Joan, my wife, made a joke of it saying things like, 'What will your dad say?' but Elisabeth wanted her photograph taken and so it was. It is a lovely picture of her, even if you can see in her chubby cheeks the effects of the cortisone. Sadly, three weeks later she died.

Both Joan and I thought it was the end of the world, at least of our world. Thankfully, it wasn't, for along came another daughter, Lena, who is now happily married and the mother of two daughters and a son.

Sadly, in August 1997, my wife Joan had a massive brain haemorrhage and died in the same hospital as Elisabeth. We had been married fifty-three years.

I, too, had medical problems in January 1965, when I suffered those chest pains which a lot of people try to dismiss as indigestion. I know I did. Then in the middle of the night I awoke drenched in perspiration with a feeling that a 16-stone man was sitting on my chest. It was my introduction to coronary thrombosis.

Painful and frightening though that introduction was, there was also a good side to it. From every crisis you learn something. There was no Intensive Care Unit in those days in the hospital to which I was taken. The cure was rest, to pop a trinitrate tablet under your tongue when you felt acute pain and to stick to the strict diet prescribed by the dieticians I secretly called the 'Beasts of Belsen'. All they asked you was, 'What would you like with your salad this evening?'

I found out why they thought I should exist on chicken and salad, one day when I was taken on a trolley to have an X-ray. A file was place on my chest and when the nurse disappeared I picked it up and began to read. In a letter to my GP the consultant had written, 'Your client is obese.' Sadly the nurse came back and snatched the file away. She told me I was not entitled to see it. I told her that if it was about me I should be allowed to read it, and I went on to say I thought it disgusting that a dreadful word like obese should have been used to describe me. I told the consultant that the following day when he came to see me. His reply was, 'We've stopped being gentle to you overweight fellows. You are obese, just over fifteen and a half stone (we hadn't heard of kilograms in those days) and we are going to change that.' Lesson No.1.

He then saw a packet of cigarettes by my bed and suggested I just had one after every meal. I asked him whether cigarettes were bad for heart trouble and he told me, 'They are worse for cardiovascular problems than they are for lung cancer.' Lesson No.2.

He then proceeded to tell me what a coronary was and what I would be able to do when I recovered. I asked about golf and he inquired about my handicap. I told him it was 20. He was all smiles. 'Don't worry, we'll have you on the golf course again as soon as you leave here,' he told me. I asked him what my handicap had to do with it and he said that if I had been a single-figure man my return to golf would have to be delayed 'because you would worry about your game. You would get het up whenever you played a bad shot. You would feel the stress more and more as your handicap got lower and lower and stress is the major cause of heart problems. But as you play off 20 you don't worry about how you play so in future just go out and enjoy yourself.' Lesson No.3.

I followed his advice, my handicap came down to 11 but now it has shot back up to a happy 18.

Before my little holiday in that Surrey hospital I had been part of another step forward by BBC Television. *Sports Special* continued to be popular but we knew there were many drawbacks to showing film of games. We wanted to use the electronic cameras. The Football League was still wary about the march of television but eventually it was agreed we could choose one match each week and call the programme *Match of the Day*. Stringent conditions were imposed: we could only show the new programme on the new network, BBC Two, which had just opened up, and the transmission had to be at half past six on Saturday evening.

So *Match of the Day* was born in 1964 and the first game was Liverpool against Arsenal at Anfield. Another condition in those days was that there had to be no mention of the game we were going to cover. This meant that *Grandstand* could not have me previewing a match at lunchtime because this would reveal where we were working. Mystified Liverpool fans saw our vans and cameras at the ground and wondered when the game was going to be shown on the box. We told them the time and then added, 'But it is on BBC Two.'

To Liverpudlians at that time BBC Two was equivalent to Television Outer Mongolia. They had never heard of it. We explained that BBC Two at the moment could be received only in the London area so there was no chance of anyone on Merseyside seeing the game. That brought up the sneers about nothing existing north of Watford according to the BBC, but a 3–2 victory for the home side made them happy, and happier still when they realized Arsenal fans would have to watch their team being beaten on the first *Match of the Day*.

Incidentally, the attendance at Liverpool was 48,000, considerably higher than BBC Two's viewing figure for the first game in what was to become in a short space of time a 'must' programme for all sports fans.

In case you ever enter a quiz competition and they ask you about the first *Match of the Day*, let me tell you that it took place on Saturday 22 August 1964. The two teams were Liverpool: Lawrence; Byrne, Moran; Milne, Yeats (captain), Stevenson; Callaghan, Hunt, Chisnall, Wallace, Thompson. Arsenal: Furnell; Howe, McCullough; Sneddon, Ure, Simpson; Armstrong, Strong, Baker, Eastham (captain), Anderson. For the benefit of younger readers, that is how the teams were set out in those days: a goalkeeper, two full backs, three half backs and five forwards.

The referee was Kenneth Howley, of Billingham. Roger Hunt scored the first *MOD* goal after only eleven minutes. Within five minutes of the second half starting, Wallace made it 2–0 and the mighty Kop began to sing 'London Bridge is falling down, poor old Arsenal'. They soon changed their tune when Arsenal scored twice in two minutes, first through Strong (who was later to join Liverpool) and then through Joe Baker, but two minutes from the end Wallace scored Liverpool's winner. Great teams score late goals.

Sooner or later *Match of the Day* had to switch to BBC One, and it did. Not only that, it was given a slot around ten o'clock on a Saturday night, much to the chagrin of the landlords of the local pubs. The programme became so popular that people used to go out for an earlier than usual drink and then get home in time to watch *MOD*.

Sadly the time slot was never rigid, and one night when it was really flexible was of the last night of the Proms. None of us minded sitting in the hot studio while the audience sang 'Rule Britannia' and 'Land of Hope and Glory' for the umpteenth time, but all that was followed by the loveable Sir Malcolm Sargent, who made the closing speech. He loved to point out what the BBC did for music – and no one could argue with that – but time went on and on and on. Soon there were whispers of, 'Come on, Malcolm, wrap it up.' Eventually he did.

At its peak *MOD* commanded an audience of 12 million or more and many of us thought that we could top that if only the powers-that-be gave the programme a starting time which was rigidly set. Today, everyone knows that 7.30 p.m. on Monday, Wednesday, Friday and Sunday is *Coronation Street* time. Nobody could be absolutely certain what was *MOD* time. And nothing has changed.

MOD has altered from its original idea. We would show highlights of the main match, with shorter highlights of the other two games we were allowed to cover, and the main match was decided only when those sitting in the editorial chair made their minds up as to which of the three games provided the most entertainment. We believed in more action and less talking. We believed the viewers wanted to see the football not listen to tactical arguments. These days the opposite seems to be true, or is it that the BBC wants us to believe that?

With *Match of the Day* safely up and running, all our thoughts turned to the 1966 World Cup, and I must admit that I wondered whether I would be there or would, because of my heart attack, be left to watch it on television rather than commentating on it. And with the aid of hindsight – it is easy to see things in their true perspective when you have that aid – I should have detected the first signs that the BBC's interest in me was not all it used to be. For instance, the only official news I got was that my contract (which guaranteed me £6,000 a year) would be held in abeyance and on my return to work it would be restarted.

Nobody made any inquiries about my progress and nobody came to see me with the exception of Cliff Michelmore, who called in twice a week on his way home after his evening programme.

Anyway, I did recover and before the end of the season I was back commentating. I didn't really notice that the BBC had not been too worried about the state of my health because we were all too excited about the forthcoming World Cup competition, which was to be played in England for the first time.

We have not been given our fair share of the major international sporting events, although we have always been very supportive of them all. Take the Olympic Games, for instance. We hosted them at the turn of the century, and again after the Second World War, when the movement was anxious to get the Games on after the wartime break. Finland, who should have hosted the 1948 Games and who were now under the control of Russia, were unable to do so. No other country felt they could cope as we all recovered from the ravages of war.

Great Britain came to the rescue. Despite the hefty bomb damage, despite the rationing, despite the fact that we were nothing like back on our feet, we rescued the Olympic Games. Without our intervention, the Olympic movement might have been cast aside on to the scrapheap. Yet we received no thanks at all. We know the 1948 Games were not perfect. How could they be? You can call the 1948 Games the Utility Games if you like, but at least we provided everyone with some excellent sport, which is what the Olympic Games is supposed to be about. Our only thanks has been that whenever a British city has applied for the Games it has been more or less ignored by all the delegates.

But the World Cup was different. It was being whispered that the Football Association was to apply for the 1966 finals and that the decision would be made some time after the 1958 competition in Sweden. Peter Dimmock, head of Outside Broadcasts at BBC Television, was determined to show FIFA how the BBC could televise the matches so he took a couple of electronic cameras and two top cameramen to Sweden and was able to give the Football Association a sample of the BBC's work to back up their application. From that moment onwards there was no doubt, England would stage the World Cup finals in 1966. They would not be the first to be televised – Switzerland in 1954, Sweden in 1958 and then Chile in 1962 had all been televised before – but 1966 would be the best final ever televised.

It was a mammoth job for the BBC and for the Independent Television companies who would join the consortium. The BBC would supply the hardware for some venues, ITV would supply the others. Both networks would cover the actual Final.

The managerial top brass of the BBC gave the sports department every assistance. Those in the sports department today must look back in envy because the real sadness of today's television is that BBC sport has been abandoned by those who control the organization known as Auntie. At least, dear old Auntie of yesteryear had some fight, some spirit.

In 1966 the BBC was top of the league when it came to sports coverage, but the World Cup was something else. Compared to today the equipment was almost prehistoric. There was, for instance, just one slow motion machine. We were given full use of it so, for the first time, slow motion replays were available at a World Cup. Mind you, the slow motion machine was light-years behind the present-day ones in technology. But, of course, we are talking about thirty-three years ago.

There were just thirty-four tape machines in the country. The BBC needed twenty-six of them. They got them. It took four riggers to carry a 280-pound camera. Today just one rigger can carry a lightweight camera in each hand. Yes, it really was the kindergarten, but not one single game in the sixteen-team World Cup 1966 was denied television coverage.

The disappointment most people felt was that the games were not in colour. We ourselves were not just disappointed: we were very angry. The BBC could have covered the 1966 World Cup in colour but we were denied by Harold Wilson's government. Two years before the tournament began the BBC told the government that colour television was possible, which would obviously enhance the coverage of such an important event. The television set manufacturers, however, claimed that they were not geared to producing the 625-line sets essential for colour television until 1967. They lobbied the government and their argument won the day, but I wonder how much it was influenced by the manufacturers wanting to get rid of their old-fashioned 425-line sets.

Just as the BBC was crafty enough to get a couple of cameras

147

into Sweden to show how good our coverage could be, so, too, we were crafty enough to prove the government wrong in 1966. There was a BBC camera on the *Radio Times* advertisement on top of the scoreboard at Wembley, towards the right of the Royal Box, and it produced splendid colour pictures of the great games the politicians denied to the country.

Even without colour television it was a great tournament and those who claim England only won because they played every game at Wembley are talking nonsense. After the first-round matches, England had to play Argentina and Portugal to reach the final, and no country would have wished for such opposition.

The quarter-final against Argentina was marred by the sending off of Rattin, the Argentine captain, and while not condoning his argumentative attitude towards the German referee I am sure matters could have been sorted out if one of the officials had been able to speak German and Spanish. The arrival on the pitch of Ken Aston, an English referee who was FIFA's referees' liaison officer, didn't help because he could not speak the two languages concerned.

But the semi-final against Portugal was a game no one will forget. Portugal were regarded as the best team in the finals, but England won. The Portuguese coach, Otto Glória, when asked after the game who would win the final, England or West Germany, said, 'But surely we saw the Final tonight.' Nobody who was at Wembley or who watched on television would disagree with him, and if Portugal had beaten England at that stage of the competition there would have been disappointment but no rancour in England.

The Final itself has been so well documented that it needs nothing more from me, except perhaps, something about England's third goal. I have seen countless pictures of the ball landing on the goal line, but they all ignore one very important fact. If a ball crosses the line in mid-air that means that a goal is awarded. The fact that the ball may not have been wholly over the line when it hit the ground is immaterial. People closest to the action are convinced the ball was well over the line in mid-air, and spectators I have spoken with who were standing behind the goal confirm that. Some even say they saw the roof of the net move.

Anyway, it all happened in 1966 and all the arguments are of no consequence because the record books show that England won 4–2.

I have heard people say that our World Cup winners were not the best England team ever. Maybe they were not, but the fact remains that they are the only eleven Englishmen to have won a competition which included national teams from all over the world. And they did it by skill, by determination, by fitness and, perhaps above all, by team spirit.

The ten players who remain alive today still comprise a team. They still keep in touch with each other, still play golf together and are still very supportive of each other. And that is because they served the finest national team manager of all time, Sir Alf Ramsey. Alf respected his players and in return earned their respect. For instance, Norbert Stiles once told me – and I use the correct name Norbert because Alf never called him Nobby – that after the semi-final victory when Alf addressed his players, he began by saying, 'Gentlemen'. Not lads, not boys, but gentlemen.

That is why the players thought the world of him. He called them gentlemen and he treated them like gentlemen. He was strict but he was always fair. He never tried to hog the limelight. He didn't jump into the air when the whistle went at the end of the final. He just took his time getting out of his seat on the bench, then he stood on the touchline and shook the hand of every player as the team walked up those famous Wembley steps to the Royal Box for Bobby Moore to receive the trophy, then called the Jules Rimet trophy, only twelve inches high, of solid gold, which meant that England were the World Champions.

The team went on the traditional lap of honour, but Alf Ramsey walked quietly to the tunnel and into the dressing-room. He was satisfied. He had done what he had said he would do the day he was appointed – win the World Cup. 'My players', as he always called the team, had done him proud. And he had done them proud.

And as George Cohen said to Lady Ramsey at the end of his address at the thanksgiving service for Sir Alf Ramsey, a service attended by all his players, 'Thank you for lending him to us.'

15

A Plot is Hatched
. . . and Foiled

The World Cup over, life got back to normal, but about two months after the victory at Wembley BBC 2 repeated the whole of the World Cup Final. It was only then that people noticed what I said as Geoff Hurst scored that all-important fourth goal. 'Some people are on the pitch. They think it's all over. It is now.'

I am still very proud that I came out with the words which fitted the action so perfectly. The only thing that hurts me is when people call it a catchphrase or, worse still, a cliché. It is neither. A catchphrase is something a comedian uses. There are loads of them, 'Nice to see you, to see you nice,' from Bruce Forsyth, for instance. And as for calling what I said a cliché, I don't see how anyone can think that.

Many people have asked me whether it was pre-planned, but I can assure you that it was not. I was lucky enough to find the right words for the moment. Mind you I once kidded a young journalist that Geoff Hurst and I worked together on the Thursday before the Final and arranged for Geoff to wear a deaf aid so that he could hear my commentary and know when to shoot. I then noticed the young lad was taking it all down in his notebook and believing every word. I felt dreadful. I apologized for kidding him along and he took it all in good part.

I am often asked if I get paid for the use of part of what I said as the title of the television show *They Think It's All Over*. The answer is an emphatic NO. I wrote to Sir John Birt, the Director General of the BBC, and asked him what the words 'they think it's all over' have to do with the programme or vice versa and he replied, 'We thought it was a good idea to bring those great words of yours to the notice of the younger people.' I almost replied that anyone who believed that would believe the earth is flat and pigs can fly.

Strangely enough there have been quite a few rumours bandied about that I never spoke those words in my commentary but that they were dubbed on to the end for the benefit of the video. Well, almost 20 million people watched the World Cup Final on BBC television so they know whether or not I said them. Nevertheless, I have had quite a few letters asking whether the dubbing story is true and I got a call from a reporter on the *Racing Times* who told me a bookmaker had definite proof that the words were added after the game. I asked the reporter to get a bet on with the bookmaker concerned. The stake didn't matter, neither did the odds. I heard no more.

On another occasion I appeared on an afternoon Radio Five Live programme hosted by John Inverdale, whom I rate as one of the finest sports presenters on radio and/or television. John Motson was on the same programme and we got a call from a man who said he had proof that I didn't say what people thought I said. He told us that his brother had a recording of the World Cup Final and I definitely did not say, 'They think it's all over' etc. John Inverdale was quick to suggest that the man got hold of the recording and call us back so that we could all hear it.

Within a quarter of an hour he was back and switched on the tape. The two Johns and I immediately cried out, 'That's the ITV commentary, not the BBC one.' Exit another loser.

The ITV commentator was Hugh Johns. If you asked them, most people would say it was Brian Moore but in 1966 Brian Moore was still a radio man and was in the BBC radio box. Hugh Johns, a good friend of mine and an experienced commentator, concentrated at the end of his commentary on Geoff Hurst's hat-trick, a feat which had never been done before in a World Cup Final and has not been done since. It was a perfectly sensible line to take and deserved ten out of ten. But sadly for Hugh it didn't ring as loud a bell as mine did.

Hugh was still the leader of the ITV commentary team in 1970 in Mexico and the BBC had arranged a party during the evening to wind up yet another World Cup. I asked Hugh if he was coming to the party and he said he hadn't been invited. Now, I know we were rivals when it came to work and the struggle to get the higher audience, but I could not see rhyme nor reason why we should not remain friends off the pitch, as it were, and socialize. So I asked Hugh to come along as my guest and he accepted. And I am delighted he did.

It wasn't all that long after the 1966 Final that someone on the BBC staff, who shall be nameless for obvious reasons, came to me and said, 'You know those words you said at the end of the World Cup Final? Well just box clever because "They think it's all over" may come true.'

I took it all with a pinch of salt and thought I had nothing to worry about when the BBC offered me a new contract on the same terms as before. The important points were that I would cover all England internationals, the FA Cup Final, the European Cup Final and the World Cup Final.

Having signed the contract I began to hear all sorts of

disturbing rumours. It was obvious that scheming little plots were going on and I heard that someone at a sportsmen's dinner in Stockport had categorically declared that I would not be the No.1 soccer commentator for the BBC in the season 1970–71.

There was nothing I could do about rumours. I was under contract and nobody had breached any of its clauses, but as week followed week I could sense the atmosphere. It is a chilling feeling. There is nothing you can really put your finger on, but you know that something sinister is going on around you. I became aware that there was a mafia-type operation going on against me. The people concerned kept a low profile but it was obvious that there was a plan afoot and I was grateful for all the bits and pieces of information my friends within the Corporation passed on to me.

At the end of the 1968–69 season, Alf Ramsey took his team on a tour to Mexico, Uruguay and Brazil. The purpose of the trip was twofold. First, he wanted his players to get accustomed to football in South and Central America, and second, he wanted to inspect the facilities in the Mexican city of Guadalajara because in the 1970 World Cup, England, as the holders, would be based there.

Two matches were arranged in Mexico. The first was a full international played in the Azteca Stadium, which would be the venue for the 1970 Final. I don't know whether the itinerary was arranged to make the players realize how tough the effects of jet lag and altitude can be, but the England squad made the long flights to Mexico City, which is almost 8,000 feet above sea level, and only three days later had to play a full ninety minutes in the blistering heat. Talking to the players afterwards, Francis Lee admitted the altitude affected him, and even Alan Ball said that the killing effect came, then went, then came again and he remembered one time when his legs just refused to move. That is quite something for Bally, as he is affectionately known, to admit.

England strolled through the game against a very poor Mexican side which had recently toured Europe winning only one of their seven matches. They even lost to Luxemburg. The vast bowl of a stadium was filled to its 120,000 capacity and England made no effort to speed up the game but their passing was always accurate. As Geoff Hurst said afterwards, 'If we can play like this now, how much better will we be next year after a month's acclimatization.'

We then moved on to Guadalajara and were allowed to turn out as an England Eleven against a Mexican Eleven. The objective was for the players to get some idea of the city and the stadium in which they would be playing all their first-round matches. We stayed in the Guadalajara Hilton and it was there that I did a television interview with Sir Alf Ramsey. He confirmed that the team would be staying in the Hilton and when I asked him whether that included the officials he gave me what I always called the 'Alf Ramsey look'. 'I shall be staying here,' he said, 'with my players and with my trainers. I neither know nor care where the officials will be staying!' So there!

After the two games in Mexico the players were subjected to another climate change. Mexico was very hot and varied from the 8,000 feet above sea level of Mexico City to the 5,000 feet of Guadalajara. The next port of call was Montevideo, the capital of Uruguay and scene of the first World Cup. Montevideo is at sea level and was in the grip of cold autumn weather. All the same England won 2–1. We had time for a little sightseeing and were taken to see where the German battleship *Graf Spey* was scuttled during the war.

Then it was on northwards to Brazil for a game in the

Maracaná stadium and the heat of Rio de Janeiro. Two late goals gave Brazil a 2–1 victory, but they looked nothing like the magnificent side we were to see in 1970.

By the time the new English season started I was still feeling uneasy. I should, I suppose, have discussed the matter with my agent and forced a showdown, but I had no evidence that my worries were justified. Then, early in 1970, the mafia struck.

Bryan Cowgill, the head of sport, asked me to go and see him, so off I went to Kensington House in Shepherds Bush. We chatted amiably enough until Bryan pulled the trigger. He said he had decided that David Coleman should get some experience of commentating on the English team, so David would cover all the England games and I would work with John McGonagle in the group in which West Germany were playing. Even though I had been suspicious for so long and been tipped off by so many people, the news was a shock. It shook me so much that I did all the wrong things, or rather failed to do the right things. I said nothing and left, when I should have said, 'Bryan, read my contract.' And then left to get in touch with my agent. There would have been an unholy row and the BBC would either have caved in or been sued for breach of contract. In either case, it meant the end of my career with BBC Television.

When I walked out of Kensington House I was so furious that I didn't even tell my agent. I had no objection to working with John McGonagle, who was a fine producer, but I had every objection to the BBC blatantly breaking my contract. With the wonderful power of hindsight I know now that I should have met fire with fire and challenged the BBC, but I didn't have that wonderful power.

*

On their way to Guadalajara for the 1970 World Cup the England team played in both Ecuador and Colombia, but I wasn't there. I flew into Guadalajara later only to find that my luggage had gone astray. I managed to track down the right man at Guadalajara airport to help me and he set things in motion while I requested and received some money from the BBC to buy the bare essentials I needed before my luggage arrived. It turned up the following day, the day I went to the airport to meet John McGonagle, whose luggage had also gone astray. But with the help of my man at the airport it was found twenty-four hours later.

The Guadalajara Hilton was a lovely hotel. It was conveniently situated, had excellent rooms, a pleasant restaurant and a large swimming pool, and I was determined to enjoy myself. I was furious at not covering any of the England games but I knew that I had a trump card up my sleeve and would have no hesitation in playing it.

John McGonagle and I got on famously, as we always did. The games we had to cover were played in León, a lovely town some distance from Guadalajara. John and I did the journey in a chauffeur-driven air-conditioned car with darkened windows, luxuries which were necessary because of the bright sunlight and intense heat. Sometimes were travelled at night which was terrifying because heavy lorries thundered along either so well lit that they looked like travelling illuminations, or with no lights at all. It was nothing to find dead cattle on the road, victims of reckless driving.

On the advice of our driver, we stopped once at a town called Tepatitlan, where we found a wonderful bar. As we walked in we saw a few men sitting drinking at a table, and as soon as they saw us they stood up, got their instruments and lo and behold we had a mariachi band. John and I ordered gin and tonics, a drink the locals had never heard of, so we promised to bring them some on our next trip. When they tried it, nobody liked it.

We used to settle for a beer or a tequila, or both, and one night after a match we gave a lift to Bryon Butler, then BBC Radio's football correspondent. He had a couple of tequilas at Tepatitlan and slept the rest of the way to Guadalajara.

One day when there was no football and nothing for us to do our driver suggested taking John and me to Tequila, the town where the drink comes from. We agreed and as we entered the town we saw many men sitting by the side of the road, heads sheltering under huge sombreros, and eyes tightly shut, as they had yet another siesta. Our driver explained that all the local families had little plots of land on which they grow the megay plant, a form of cactus which takes three years to grow, from which tequila is distilled. The peasants wait patiently until their plants have matured and then they sell them to the distillery. They then buy more plants, sow them, and live on the rest of the money for the following three years, until the next crop is ready.

Our driver drove us right inside the distillery. We said we should ask someone's permission to look over the factory, but the Mexican just laughed. So we were shown how tequila is distilled. As we were leaving, we met two of the directors, who were delighted to see us and told us not to pay more than ten English shillings for a bottle of tequila. With that advice they gave the pair of us a bottle of tequila which had aged for ten years in an oak cask before being bottled. Believe it or not, it was the colour of whisky.

John and I were keen to visit one of the many bars in Tequila so we did. Hygiene was certainly not of great importance. Once the tequila was poured the barman picked up a block of ice, hit it with a hammer and then picked up a couple of pieces of ice and dropped them into our glasses. We both drank a toast to the anti-Montezuma's Revenge tablets with which we had been issued.

I was so taken with León that with Alan Prentice as cameraman and Fred Clarke as sound recordist I did a little feature on the town. The funniest thing we came across was a road sign a few miles outside the town, which pointed both right and left and told us León was five kilometres away.

The town was en fête for the World Cup. Streets, shops and houses were decorated and there was dancing every night in the main square opposite the Hotel Condessa, where the Moroccan team were staying. The people were terribly friendly and they just loved the Moroccans, whose manager was Blagoje Vidinic, a former Yugoslav goalkeeper whom I had seen play many times. He told me that although every country was allowed twenty-two players in their squad, he could only find nineteen good enough to make the trip. They were all amateurs, a mixture of Parachute Regiment officers, Army musicians, male nurses, farm workers and civil servants. And to think that they had to play West Germany in their very first game. But they took the lead after twenty minutes, held it for thirty-five minutes and were only beaten by a late goal in the second half.

It was in León that John and I realized how low in the BBC pecking order we had become. As we were leaving to cover our first match we were told that no accommodation had been booked for us in León, but if we contacted the German television people they had spare rooms. We did, and they hadn't. So we had to scout around and try to find somewhere to stay in the friendly little town. I think we slept in every hotel in the town.

Then John developed the dreaded Montezuma's Revenge. As he lay in bed in a darkened room I had to make sure he took the right dose of pills at the right time. He didn't make much progress, in fact he didn't seem to make any and when we were breaking into my stock of pills I sent a message to Jack Oaten, who was in charge of administration at the headquarters in Guadalajara. I said that if more medication and medical help wasn't sent within twenty-four hours I was going to get the best and most expensive doctor in León to attend John. That did the trick.

John McGonagle never made a complete recovery from this illness while in Mexico. The Mexicans claim that when Montezuma takes his revenge on you then you never upset him again. However, when the games in León ended, we wended our way back to Guadalajara, where the heat and the sun really did cause problems.

The television pundits back home kept on about the altitude, but that was no problem. Everyone, players and media people, had acclimatized so we knew how to pace ourselves and how to cope with the altitude. The sun was a much bigger problem, but the experts back home who had never been to Mexico, let alone Guadalajara, didn't bother about that. They rambled on about the altitude of only 5,000 feet. So much for pundits sitting in comfortable studios thousands of miles away from the action.

The photographers suffered the most. They found it difficult to get the right setting on their lenses. The English players suffered too, and all because they were transported in the wrong bus. It was a bus that had been brought from England and its idea of air-conditioning was to draw the outside hot air into the coach and blow it round the interior of the vehicle. This had the players puffing and sweating. Nor were the windows screened against the rays of the sun.

Always travelling behind that England bus was another vehicle carrying all the kit. That second bus had been loaned by the Mexicans, who gave one to every team. So we had the ludicrous situation of the players sweating and shielding their eyes while their kit travelled in the luxury of proper air-conditioning and screened windows.

As the tournament went on I still had my deep suspicions that I would be told that I was not going to do the commentary on the Final. I was, of course, determined that I would, and to make sure of that I had, before leaving for Mexico, shown my contract to a solicitor friend of mine. After reading it, he told me there was no way the BBC could offer the 1970 World Cup Final to anyone else, always providing I was fit and able to commentate. As a great believer in using the belt and braces technique in circumstances like this, I asked the solicitor to take Counsel's advice. His report also indicated that the contract was watertight.

So we devised a plan. The *Radio Times* is delivered to BBC staff before it appears in the bookstalls, and I arranged with a friend of mine to make sure than an advance copy was sent to my solicitor. He was then to telephone me in Mexico and confirm that my name was in the *Radio Times* as the commentator.

Eventually the telephone call arrived. I was told that there was a big spread about the Final on page 24 of the *Radio Times*, which in those days cost ninepence. Across the top of the page were six pictures of Geoff Hurst scoring the fourth goal in the 1966 Final. The caption: '1966 . . . World Cup Final . . . the goal that really, really nailed it. Hurst, chased by a German defender, lets go with a shot which rockets under the bar . . . it's all over! World Cup Final 1970 . . . join David Coleman in the great bowl of the Azteca Stadium for football's greatest drama.'

To say I was fuming is putting it mildly.

I was even more furious when the whole billing was read to me:

6.00 p.m.: The 1970 World Cup Final. Introduced by David Coleman from Mexico. The whole of the world's greatest football occasion as it happens in the Azteca Stadium, Mexico City. David Coleman sets the scene in the Azteca Stadium as the crowd of over 100,000 gathers for the world's most important football occasion.

6.10 p.m. All the latest news from Mexico with comment and analysis by the *Grandstand* team of experts, including Joe Mercer and Don Revie.

6.20 p.m. Meet the finalists.

6.50 p.m. The World Cup Final. The whole match as it happens in the Azteca Stadium. With action reply of the game's outstanding moments and expert analysis by David Coleman and the *Grandstand* team.

Nothing could be plainer. The marriage between Kenneth Wolstenholme and the BBC was not just on the rocks, it was finished for all time. And finished in the most deplorable, insulting way. As my solicitor said, 'Your name doesn't appear anywhere in the magazine.'

One thing delayed the break-up, but it was only a delay, not a saviour. It was England's 3–2 defeat against West Germany after they had been leading 2–0.

16

The Parting of the Ways

England's defeat was a bitter blow to the BBC and I can imagine the discussions in the Television Centre between Paul Fox and his head of Sport, Bryan Cowgill. David wouldn't be too keen on doing a commentary on two foreign sides. After all, the BBC had decided that he should follow the England team during the build-up and duration of the competition for one reason only: so that he could do the commentary on the Final. Now England were out and on their way home, so why not delay the *coup de grâce* for Wolstenholme until the end of his contract in a year's time?

That is obviously what they decided and why I did my fifth World Cup Final commentary. And what a brilliant game on which to finish my World Cup career. Both teams played magnificently and although it didn't have the nationalistic feeling of the '66 Final, it really was a game to remember.

It was sad that England could not retain the trophy, but that's football, and I must admit I love the story Jack Charlton tells of the sad early trip back home. Jack had been thinking long and hard about his international career and had come to the conclusion that his days in the England team were over. He had decided to tell Alf how he felt to sound out his opinion.

Noticing that there was an empty seat next to Alf on the aeroplane, Jack went and sat there. He said to Alf, who was reading a newspaper, 'Alf, I've enjoyed playing for England, but I'm well into my thirties so I think I would be wise if I called it a day.' Sir Alf Ramsey lowered his newspaper, said, 'I totally agree, Jack.' Then picked up his newspaper and continued reading. That was typical of Sir Alf.

Gradually, we all drifted back to England and before we knew where we were another football season was upon us. I didn't enjoy it after my encounter with the dirty tricks brigade.

It was blatantly obvious that this was my last season with the BBC. My contract was up at the end of the season and I could see no chance whatsoever that the Corporation would offer me another one. After all, if they had been so keen to break the contract in the middle of a World Cup, there was no way they were going to play the gentleman's game in the future.

What the BBC didn't realize is that if England had reached the final they would have been presented with an injunction preventing them from transmitting the game and there would subsequently have been a claim for breach of contract. I am sure that this would have shaken the top brass of the BBC because I think the force against me consisted of just two people, Paul Fox and Bryan Cowgill. Both were determined, for reasons known only to themselves, to make David Coleman the commentator supreme. He would be allowed to take over any sport he wished.

I am convinced that people like Alec Weeks, Sam Leitch and John McGonagle had inklings of what was going on but I don't think any of them were part of the plot. Even Peter Dimmock was unaware of the situation. Three times since I left the BBC he has said to me that I should not have held out for more money. If I hadn't done, I would have become one of the highly paid commentators. The fact is that I never did hold out for more money. Money was never a subject of contention. That Peter Dimmock should think it was points very sharply to the fact that he was unaware of what was going on.

Late in the autumn of 1998 the BBC celebrated the fortieth anniversary of *Grandstand* with a lunch at Ascot racecourse because it so happened that racing at Ascot was the be-all and end-all of *Grandstand* that Saturday.

I accepted the invitation to attend even though I had to hobble into the racecourse with the aid of a stick, wearing a bedroom slipper on my left foot, the result of having damaged the hamstring in my left leg. It was great to meet so many old friends and I had a long chat with Peter Dimmock. He reiterated that he was sorry I had left the BBC because I was far and away the best football commentator they had. It was on the tip of my tongue to tell him why I did leave, but I thought it was neither the time nor the place. It will harm nobody if Peter thinks I left because I wanted more money.

The final crunch came towards the end of the 1970–71 season. I received a telephone call from Bryan Cowgill asking me to attend a meeting in the Television Centre in Wood Lane, London. As we were approaching the end of the season I thought it was the usual planning meeting we had before the FA Cup Final, so I readily agreed to attend.

When I got there I was surprised to see Paul Fox because he was no longer in Sport. He had progressed, through Current Affairs, to one of the highest positions in BBC Television. Bryan Cowgill was there as head of Sport, but I was intrigued there was no Alex Weeks, the director, the man in charge of televising the Cup Final. Any meeting without him would be useless if we were going to discuss the coverage of the forthcoming Cup Final.

We were going to do exactly that. Only with a difference. I am not sure whether it was Paul or Bryan who spoke first, but as they were close allies it doesn't matter. What does matter is what was said. And the words were, 'We are going to have David Coleman instead of you as the commentator at the Cup Final.'

At that moment I should have excused myself as politely as possible and walked out. It was most unethical for two representatives of the BBC to discuss future policy towards an artist without the artist's agent being present. I knew Bryan Cowgill couldn't stand Sheelagh O'Donovan, who represented me in those days, but that didn't excuse either him or Paul for wanting a discussion without the agent's presence. But I was so shocked at the opening remarks that I made the error of staying.

Paul Fox was a shrewd operator whereas Bryan Cowgill always tended to blow his top, and Bryan shouted when I pointed out that I had a contract which gave me the right to the Cup Final. He said they could get round that if needs be by letting me do the commentary on the recording they made on tape and sent all round the world, while David would be doing the live commentary. If looks could kill, he would have dropped dead there and then.

Paul tried to be more diplomatic when I brought up the question of the 1970 World Cup and had the decency to admit that if England had reached the 1970 Final I would not have done the commentary, David Coleman would have. By this time we were approaching the bare-knuckles and no-holds-barred stage so I snapped, 'If I hadn't been the commentator the BBC would not have transmitted the game.' I left them to work that out for themselves, which I don't suppose they did.

Paul Fox assured me he wanted me to continue working for the BBC and he was willing to offer me another three-year contract with a 'but' attached to it. The 'but' was that the contract would not include the most important clause of the previous ones, the clause which gave me the right to be the No.1 commentator, to cover all the England games, the FA Cup Final, the European Cup Final and the World Cup Final. As a sweetener, my guarantee would be increased from £6,000 a year to £9,000. But the whole plan was a David Coleman takeover.

I made it absolutely plain that there was no way I would sign a contract that had the most important clause deleted and that I had no intention of becoming just a journeyman commentator, being fed scraps of the jobs. With that I got up and left.

I felt angry. I felt humiliated. I felt insulted. And I think that the BBC behaved in a despicable fashion. Even though most of the people within the BBC would not have agreed with the actions of the two men who had engineered the whole sordid business, nevertheless the BBC was tainted by their actions. It is ironical that David soon got fed up with commentating on football and handed over the job to the new boy, John Motson.

The first thing I did when I got out of that meeting room was use one of the public call boxes in the foyer of Television Centre to speak to Sheelagh O'Donovan. She could not believe what she was hearing. She was annoyed that I had been lured to a meeting thinking it was to plan the coverage of the Cup Final when Paul Fox and Bryan Cowgill knew all along it was to discuss my future (such as it was) with the BBC.

Sheelagh went into the attack straightaway. Within the space of a few days the BBC was forced to capitulate and I did the FA Cup Final. I would imagine that the contracts department made it clear to Messrs Fox and Cowgill that in no way could they allow a contract to be broken in the way the two suggested.

But the BBC would not budge on the terms of the renewal of

my contract, and neither would I. However much money they offered me I would not agree to a contract which I thought was an insult. Many people inside the BBC pleaded with me and said I could not throw away twenty-three years with the BBC just like that. I replied that if the BBC thought so little of my twenty-three years' work for them there was no reason why I should stay with a downgraded contract.

Happily for me, UEFA (the European Football Union) had decided that the 1971 European Cup Final should be played at Wembley Stadium, and it was with much relief that I found out that the BBC was not going to try another little prank to steer me away from the commentary box.

The game was between Ajax from Holland and Panathinaikos from Greece, and it is a pleasure to report that both clubs had won their national championship the season before and were, therefore, justifiably entitled to play in the European Cup. Those were the happy days before the competition was downgraded and renamed the European Champions' Cup. The snag is that now it is not only national champions that take part but runners-up and, in some cases, teams who finished no better than fourth in their national pecking order. As I write this, we have just experienced an unforgettable final between Manchester United and Bayern Munich, two great clubs, although neither of them should have been allowed into the competition in the first place for the simple reason that they were not the champions of their respective countries.

In 1971 it was good to see Ferenc Puskas, that legend of Hungarian football, lead Panathinaikos on to the field as their manager. Wembley would have wonderful memories of him, of the 1953 international match between Hungary and England which Hungary won 6–3, so becoming the first non-British country to beat England at Wembley. No doubt Puskas glanced at the goal to the right of the Royal Box and smiled as he remembered the incredible goal he scored at that end on that murky November afternoon eighteen years earlier.

This time, however, Puskas was on the bench and unable to work his magic out there on the playing pitch. His team tried their best but they were not able to cope with the beautiful Ajax side which played what became known as 'total football'. They won 2–0 – first of their three consecutive European Cup victories.

Wembley held memories for me, too, as I sat in the commentary box high in the stand for what I knew to be the last time as a BBC man. I could share Puskas's memories of that dull November afternoon in 1953 when the Hungarians showed us that the game we had been playing was not football. Then there was the boring memory of that Charlton Athletic *v.* Burnley Cup Final which would have been completely forgotten by everyone if it hadn't been for Chris Duffy's goal and his hilarious celebrations. And the heart-breaking memory of 1953 (yes, the year of the Hungarians) when Bolton Wanderers led Blackpool 3–1 with only some fifteen minutes of the FA Cup Final remaining, but managed to lose it 3–4. It was called the Stanley Matthews final, no doubt became it was the first time Stan had been on the winning side in a final, though some people queried why it was called the Matthews Final when Stan Mortensen had scored a hat-trick in the game.

This remark was recalled at Stan Mortensen's funeral when someone said, 'Morty gets a hat-trick in the Cup Final and they call it the "Matthews Final". Now we are burying Morty, do we call this the "Matthews Funeral"?' Actually Mortensen didn't score a hat-trick, although the official records credit him with one. But anyone sitting in the Royal Box stand could see that the shot which brought one of the goals was going well wide until it hit Harold Hassall, of Bolton, and flew into the far corner of the net. But Morty has now left us so let's not mess about with the record books.

It was a strange feeling when the final whistle went, the presentation ceremony ended and I handed back to the studio. It was all over, twenty-three years finished, just like that. Of course I was sad. Who wouldn't be? I had twenty-three years of the best job in the world, doing what I loved doing, and now it had ended. Not through any wish of mine but just because a carefully laid plan had been devised to make sure I was pushed aside.

The crew were marvellous. Every single one of them came to shake my hand and wish me well. They told me they couldn't understand why it had all finished the way it had. I went into the scanner for a few minutes, but then it was time to go and I just walked to my car and drove home.

You could say that I could have stayed, accepted the increased money I was offered and maybe, when David Coleman got fed up with covering football, I could have been back in the old position. I don't agree. The idea was to get rid of me and if I had agreed to the new contract it would have been the last one I would have been offered. And the humiliation I would have suffered would have been sickening.

I thought back to the coronary thrombosis days when no one, except Cliff Michelmore, came to see me, no one inquired how I was getting on and I didn't receive a single get well card from the people who engineered my downfall. Similarly, when I left I did not receive a single official letter of thanks from the BBC. I contrasted that with the fact that people who had worked on

Grandstand in whatever capacity were presented with a memento in the shape of a replica of the Sports Personality of the Year award. Not that I wanted a replica, but a letter would have been nice.

People have often asked me what on earth I did when I left the BBC. It amazed me that there were those who believed that if you were not seen regularly on the box you were either dead or in an old people's home. So few believe that there is life after the BBC.

I did very well, thank you. First of all, my old pal Frank Nicklin, then the sports editor of the *Sun*, thought it would be a good idea if I kept up the *Match of the Day* tradition and reported the game for the *Sun*. The only snag was that in those days the programme's main match had to be kept under wraps. It was an official secret, but where there are official secrets there are moles and I had one within the BBC. As soon as I knew which the big match was going to be that week, I telephoned Frank Nicklin and, hey presto, I was sitting in the right press box come three o'clock the following Saturday.

That lasted one season. The gimmick couldn't go on any longer because it would have lost its attraction, so I switched back to television and worked for Tyne Tees Television. I enjoyed that immensely, despite the fact that their equipment left a lot to be desired. For instance, when I was there they had no slow motion machine.

The coverage didn't go far and wide. Newcastle United were the big club, followed by Middlesbrough and Sunderland, and it was always fun going to Hartlepool and Darlington. The ground at Hartlepool is next door to an indoor bowling rink and people used to joke that there were more people watching the bowling than would be watching the football. But one season when the Pool were drawn at home against Aston Villa in the

League Cup, it was announced that anyone who turned up on Saturday for the home league game would be guaranteed a ticket for the Villa game. Hartlepool got a bumper gate that Saturday.

At Darlington, a friendly and welcoming club despite being desperately short of money, the ritual after the game was a couple of drinks in the boardroom and then a quick dash to the adjacent cricket club for another drink. With one eye on the clock, it was another quick dash by taxi to the station for the London train. In those days you stood a good chance of finding a dining-car on the train. If you were lucky you would meet John Arlott (in the dining-car, of course), in which case it would mean a generous amount of claret before arrival at King's Cross.

Newcastle United was the most convenient because it was only a short walk to the station, and across the road from the ground was one of those clubs where the fans used to gather before matches. Times were hard on Tyneside in those days but nothing could dampen the love for football. The plan in the club was that a few fellows each put a little money into a kitty, which would be sufficient to buy a Federation Ale or Newcastle Brown or two and have a little over for a flutter on the horses.

Those folk in the north-east are the salt of the earth. They have endured the bad times and enjoyed the good times but they have always loved 'our team'. They would criticize them if they were playing badly – and Newcastle did a lot of playing badly in those days – but if an outsider was daft enough to utter a single word against the Magpies, they would run the risk of being the object of a little aggro.

The Geordies didn't want to win at any cost. They wanted to win by sheer footballing skill. One Saturday I got talking to a group of Newcastle supporters as I waited for my train at the station, when one lad claimed that Jinky Smith had been the man of the match. I said that was nonsense, he was only in the game for about four minutes. 'Yes,' was the reply, 'only four minutes but four minutes of sheer genius and sheer delight.'

That is how the Geordies like their football. A little bit of brilliance is better than a lot of just honest endeavour. And, of course, Newcastle fans regard the club down the road, called Sunderland, as just cannon fodder for them.

Sunderland fans are fantastic, and I have a great admiration for their manager, Peter Reid. He had a terrific start in his footballing life: he played for Bolton Wanderers. And if you think I am biased, yes I am. I want to see Sunderland's new Stadium of Light soon to erase my memories of Roker Park, their old ground. Roker Park was designated a World Cup ground for 1966 and the television position was on top of the stand opposite the main stand. Commentators were never consulted about television positions but the riggers were always concerned (quite rightly) about how to get the heavy equipment into position. At Roker Park they were faced with a roof which sloped steeply upwards and then down on to the permanent television position. As the equipment was so heavy they had to haul it up by ropes, so they asked that a smooth surface ramp be put on top of the stand.

Thank you, fellows. It made life easier for you, but it terrified me. To reach the commentary position I had to walk upwards on this steep, smooth ramp, clinging tightly to the railing on one side because one slip meant . . . well, we don't talk about that. Getting down was even worse because when I got to the apex of the roof I was faced with coming down this smooth ramp and staring into a drop of what seemed like . . . well, one slip and that would have been it.

I knew the then Sunderland chairman, Syd Collings, very

well and he told me the club was proud of the television position. I asked him if he had every been up there and he said, 'Not likely.' And I don't blame him.

If Sunderland had the most scary television in the north-east, Middlesbrough had the most difficult journey back to London from their old Ayresome Park ground. Most times it was a hired car to Darlington, with a helpful police motor cycle escort to guide us through the heavy traffic around the ground. Sometimes, though, I could get a lift from the visiting team. Once Southampton were the visitors and they played very badly. After the match they were flying back from Teesside airport and so was I. Their manager, Lawrie McMenemy, offered me a lift which I accepted most gratefully. Not far from Teesside airport there is a horrible-looking factory. Disappointed with his team's performance, Lawrie pointed to the dreadful sight and said to his players, 'Any more performances like the one this afternoon and you'll all have to do a week's work in that place for no wages.' I am sure Southampton never played as badly again.

Having spent so long in the RAF I was still interested in aviation so gladly accepted the opportunity in the late seventies of doing some work for British Caledonian. Sadly the company was up against the very powerful British Airways and eventually was swallowed by the big fish. But whenever I flew with them, first as British United Airways, of which Freddie Laker was the boss, and later as British Caledonian, led by Adam Thompson, I found them an excellent airline. That opinion didn't change when I worked for them.

I remember going to Rio de Janeiro with them to watch a tournament at which all the referees were from England. We were relaxing on Copacabana Beach one morning and the usual traders came along trying to sell their worthless goods. We managed to get rid of them, but we had not watched out for their accomplice, who had carefully successfully removed the money from the trousers of one of the referees as he lay on the beach sunbathing and watching those Brazilian beauties, who are just as gorgeous on Copacabana Beach as they are at Ipanema.

One day in 1972 I was approached by Jarvis Astaire and Mickey Duff to see if I would take over the secretaryship of the Anglo-American Sporting Club, an organization which ran boxing-dinner evenings in London at the Park Lane Hilton and in Manchester at the Hotel Piccadilly, which is now part of the Jarvis Hotels Group. My job was to greet the guests of honour, which gave me the opportunity of meeting great sporting idols of the day, such as Mohammed Ali and Mike Tyson, politicians like Harold Wilson, and countless personalities from all walks of life. In Manchester we often had as the main speaker Canon Reg Smith of Bury. In his younger days he was a great sports-man and he later became vice chairman of the Bury Football Club. He was a tremendous speaker, who would always end a sincere Grace by saying, 'And bless, please, My Lord, all we sinners who haven't paid for our dinner.'

Most of the boxing was professional, but there were some great amateur nights and we had one tremendous battle between the British Combined Services and the United States Marine Corps. I remember briefing the two team managers that the teams should march in behind their flag and stand in the ring for the playing of the national anthems, with the United States anthem being first as they were the visitors. The two flags, I said, would be lowered in salute as each anthem was played.

That plan was vetoed by the United States team leader. 'The

United States Marines flag is never lowered,' he said. I asked him whether it is ever lowered as a mark of respect for a national anthem and he answered, 'No, sir. The Marines never lower the flag.'

So, no flags were lowered.

All the functions at the Anglo-American Sporting Club were for men only. One day when we were again presenting a Britain *v.* American Services boxing match, I was asked by one of the American officers whether it would be all right if their team doctor sat at ringside. I said of course it would and thought no more of it.

It turned out that the American team doctor was a very attractive lady, dressed in the same uniform as the male officers. I for one was glad she was with us.

I must admit that I never found I had time on my hands. In 1974 I was invited to join the golf committee at the Royal Automobile Golf & Country Club at Woodcote Park in Epsom, where I had been a member since 1955. I was looking forward to serving on the golf committee until I discovered that the club was in a parlous state financially, so much so that it was in danger of being sold.

We all realized that a good offer would get Woodcote Park, but there were one or two snags. There were some listed buildings and there was no chance of the huge acreage being allowed to be developed. So a number of the prospective buyers lost interest.

Thank goodness they did because gradually the club started to find its feet again after a complete revamping of the committees. The real comeback was started under chairmanship of Jeffrey Rose and now the club is second to none in prosperity. The premises and facilities at the Pall Mall clubhouse are magnificent and you could not ask for a better country club than the one at Woodcote Park, with a splendid clubhouse and accommodation, two 18-hole golf courses and an excellent leisure centre with a swimming pool and tennis and squash courts.

But during my seven years on the golf committee, which included one year as captain, we were struggling, though during my year of office as captain we hosted the Martini Professional tournament. Rank has it privileges and I was privileged to play with Seve Ballesteros in the Pro-Am.

All we hacker golfers dream of a moment of glory on the golf course, such as a hole in one, which I have never achieved. My moment came at the short 13th hole in the Pro-Am. With my tee shot I was slightly inside Seve's ball. That would have done for me. You know the feeling . . . the day I got inside Seve Ballesteros's tee shot on a par three. But more was to come. I marked my ball and watched as Seve's putt lipped the hole and stayed out. Mine was a difficult putt, not so much because of the distance but because my hands kept shaking and my legs were wobbling. At long last I stroked the ball with my putter and, would you believe it, the ball dropped in for a birdie two. I had outplayed the great Ballesteros. All right, so it was only on one hole, but . . . well, never mind what happened afterwards. All I can say is that the great man played like the genius he was.

Golf has always been a passion with me and I love playing in the charity events, such as Frankie Vaughan's days for the boys' clubs at Hazelmere in Buckinghamshire, Harry Carpenter's for the same charity at Wentworth, Stephanie Moore's at Wentworth in aid of the Bobby Moore Cancer Fund, all the days in aid of SPARKS at various courses, and the day in aid of the

Foundation for Children with Leukaemia when we play with golf club captains at Wentworth.

There is also one at Mere in Cheshire run by the firm of Willie Morgan, the former Manchester United, Bolton Wanderers and Burnley international footballer. It is the Howard Keel classic in aid of the NSPCC. It is always superbly organized and the highlight is the dinner after the golf when we are entertained to a top-notch cabaret. It was at one of these that I achieved another ambition: I sang with Howard Keel. Well, it wasn't just me but . . . anyway, here's the story.

At the end of the show, Howard Keel went on stage to tell us that he remembered with great pleasure his first appearance in Manchester, and he added, 'I am delighted that you have taken to your hearts the hit song I sang in the show. You have made it your football anthem. But you don't sing the right words. You keep singing "When you walk through a storm hold your head up high." But those are not the right words.'

He called all the celebrities who had played golf in the golf day up to the stage and we sang the *right* words, which are, 'When you walk through a storm hold your *chin* up high.'

The word 'great' is the most over-used word in the English language. We are all guilty. Writers, television commentators and presenters and the man and woman in the street. So many things and people we call 'great' are not great. They are very good but not great. Howard Keel, though, *is* great. I first met him when he played the London Palladium and a television magazine thought we looked like each other and wanted a photo of us together. We met, shook hands, he was charming and we had our pictures taken together. They were later published in the magazine with the caption, 'Howard Keel is a dead ringer for Kenneth Wolstenholme.' No magazine has been more complimentary to me.

We didn't meet again until the first time I played in his golf classic at Mere. There is a private party at the Hotel Piccadilly on the Saturday night and when Howard Keel walked in I just gasped. The whole atmosphere changed. He is a real star, a man who can capture an audience without having to do anything at all. There is nothing boastful about him. He is a perfect gentleman. And what a voice he still has.

So there was life for me after the BBC. Though I always felt that my name had been crossed off the Christmas card list by BBC Television, especially the sports department, I even worked for the Corporation sometimes.

Then, one day I read a paragraph in a daily newspaper.

17

A Change of Direction

The small paragraph in the newspaper announced that Channel Four were to televise a game every Sunday from Italy's First Division or, as the Italians call it, Serie A. That interested me so I telephoned Michael Grade, then the head of Channel Four. He confirmed the story but told me that Channel Four would have nothing to do with the production which would be in the hands of an independent production company called Chrysalis. He advised me to get in touch with the managing director of Chrysalis Sport, a gentleman called Neil Duncanson.

I wrote Neil a letter and before I knew what I was doing I was sitting in his office in the Chrysalis headquarters in Bramley Road, just a long goal kick away from the BBC's Television Centre in Wood Lane. He told me that the idea was to produce a Saturday morning programme called *Gazetta Football Italia* giving news of what is happening in Italian football circles and reports of the previous Sunday matches. Then on the Sunday, *Football Italia* would consist of a live game from Italy. Peter Brackley had already been signed to do the commentaries but Neil wanted me to work on both programmes, and we shook hands on a deal.

Never for one moment have I regretted doing so. Chrysalis Sport was a new, young company and remains fresh to this day. It has no prima donnas. If the telephone rings, someone will pick it up and help the caller. It is, in short, a happy company and it is a pleasure to work for it.

The Chrysalis Group plc, its parent company, has been in existence for some time. It was started by the present chairman, Chris Wright, who got into the music business when he was at Manchester University, arranging gigs for many of the under-graduate bands and transporting them to and from their engagements in his old van.

After university, Chris set up a music publishing company which he later sold. Now he has branched out into all areas of the entertainment world. Chrysalis is big in commercial radio, with stations all over the country. It has a large number of artistes under its wing, a big music library, many production companies and, of course, Chrysalis Sport.

Chris Wright is a sports fan himself and fairly recently bought both Queen's Park Rangers and the Wasps Rugby Union team, placing them both under the banner of a new company, Loftus Road plc, which is not part of the Chrysalis group. Chris Wright believed that in the present harsh financial world of modern sport it made commercial sense to have both teams playing on the same ground, in one stadium. The experiment has not been as successful as it was hoped, mainly because Queen's Park Rangers have not been having a happy time.

I remember that just after Chris Wright bought Rangers – in fact, I think it was the first match under his ownership – they played Bolton Wanderers at Loftus Road. The score was 1–1 as the referee got ready to blow the final whistle. But Bolton were quicker than the referee. John McGinlay, of Bolton, sent a square pass along the edge of the penalty area and Alan

Thompson shot low into the corner of the net. Bolton won 2–1. I was pleased, Chris Wright was not.

It didn't take me long to decide that not only was it pleasant to work for the Chrysalis Group but also that it would be sensible to invest some money in it. So I did. I am not going to tell you how much and what price I paid for the shares, but I am doing very nicely, thank you.

Yet at first glance investors might not be attracted to Chrysalis. They don't announce huge profits each year, nor do they pay huge dividends. That might not be good for some people who are looking for a large annual income, but Chrysalis has continued with a sensible policy of investing its money back into the company. This has meant that they have been able to open more commercial radio stations, build up other businesses and as a result the share price has risen steadily although the balance sheet reports losses.

The expansion of Chrysalis Sport is a good example of new strategy. *Football Italia* became perhaps the flagship, but under the dynamic leadership of Neil Duncanson, and with people such as Steve Gowans and Mike Williams, the Italian football programmes have become slicker, more professional and captured larger audiences. In fact the Sunday afternoon viewing figures compare favourably with Sky's for the Premiership match.

I have mentioned three people with whom I have been closely associated, but the staff has grown like Topsy, and it has grown because Chrysalis Sport has produced so many other programmes. They moved a complete team to the United States to cover the national basketball season and they picked up the plum job of producing the Formula One programmes for ITV when they won the rights from the BBC.

On top of that they have produced programmes for the minor

182

sports, and I use that expression with great trepidation because one of those minor sports is fishing, and I know that nothing annoys the fishing fraternity more than to hear their sport being called 'minor'. After all, there are more active participants in fishing than in any other sport in the United Kingdom. But television regards fishing as a minor sport because there isn't enough action and it takes a lot of hard work to make a fishing programme interesting to a wide audience. There have been successes when people such as Gareth Edwards or Jack Charlton have fronted the programme, but it is hard to give a fishing programme the kick it needs. Fishing is a very private sport, isn't it?

But Chrysalis has succeeded and it says a lot for the planning and technique of Chrysalis Sport when you discover they can cover successfully not only the mass appeal sports of football and Formula One but also sports such as fishing and indoor bowls. I have been involved only with the football programmes, which are difficult enough, but I have always admired the versatility of the staff who are able to cover fishing and bowls and make a great success of them.

The big day for *Gazetta Football Italia* is Friday. The editors have cut the highlights of all the Serie A games and also the commentary match from the previous Sunday. James Richardson has scouted through the Italian papers, and there are lots of them, and put his review of them on film. He will also have conducted on film an interview with a leading figure in Italy. Someone will have gone over from England on Thursday to pick up all the film and bring it back to London the following day. It is then rushed to the editing suites at the Todd AO studios in Camden Town, which for the whole of Friday is the hub of *Gazetta Football Italia*. And when I say the whole of Friday I mean it because it isn't far off midnight when the editors call it a day and are happy that everything has been put in its right place for the transmission on Saturday morning.

Channel Four obviously took a risk in buying the United Kingdom rights for Italian football. They must have known that there are people in the UK who feel that Italian football is not as fast or as exciting as the English game. They must have known, too, that it might, perhaps, be difficult to get British people to be as passionate about Italian clubs and players as about their own.

Previous attempts to interest viewers in foreign sport failed largely because the coverage was not in depth. It is not enough to show a sporting event, say, once a week and leave it at that. It is essential to get the viewers interested in the teams and the players and this is what Chrysalis have done with Italian football. Viewers have realized that the quality of football in Serie A is higher than anything at home. Pundits like Alan Hansen, a classic player himself in his day, have admitted that Serie A is light years ahead of the Premiership when it comes to the real skills, and it is significant that since Chrysalis began their two programmes there has been an influx of Italian players into our game, but there has been no rush by the Italians to sign British footballers.

To the credit of our players – past and present – they have become fans of *Gazetta Football Italia* and *Football Italia*. They watch both programmes, which complement each other, and the interest in, and knowledge of, Italian football here at home has increased season on season. The decision to produce two programmes rather than be content with showing just the Sunday live match was the trump card. As their knowledge of what is happening in Italy has increased, British fans have become fans of Italian clubs and they follow their favourite Italian clubs just as avidly as they follow the home favourites.

This has manifested itself in many ways, with supporters' clubs of the leading Italian teams being formed in Britain. The Viola Club of London, supporters of Fiorentina, was probably the first but others have followed. Tour operators have realized the growing interest in Italian football and run trips to Italy for aficionados who want to go to matches. People who cannot get across to Italy seek out places where they can watch the games on television. One London coffee bar has the satellite equipment to show three games at a time in different rooms. The sale of replica Italian football shirts in the UK is booming. The magazine, *Football Italia*, edited by John D. Taylor, has become ever more popular because of the widespread coverage it gives to the Italian game, both Serie A and Serie B.

So thanks to the enterprise of Channel Four and the professionalism of Chrysalis Sport production, Italian football has become a cult in Britain, the home of football. Sadly, viewers in Wales are not served so well because, despite the large percentage of people of Italian extraction who are resident in Wales, their television company does not take *Football Italia*. Disappointed viewers complain to Chrysalis and to *Football Italia* magazine when they should complain to Welsh Television.

18

Television Today

Television has come a long way since it reappearance after the war just over fifty years ago. From a promising infant it has grown to be a huge giant, the biggest entertainment and information vehicle the world has ever known. At first it was timid and grateful for any help it could get. Today it has developed such power that it wellnigh controls the sports which tried to hinder its progress from the very beginning.

So much has changed. In days gone by the television equipment was bulky and cumbersome; today it is lightweight and easily handled. With so many satellites scurrying around in the sky above, the world has contracted and television pictures can be transmitted to and from the most inaccessible places in the world.

Sport is the jewel in the television crown. That has meant a lot to the major sports, such as football, rugby, cricket, snooker, boxing, tennis and Grand Prix motor racing, though considerably less to some of the sports which were the bread and butter of television in the early days. No one can get away with a diet of show jumping, all-in wrestling and swimming today. They were the darlings of the television companies in the past but they have been almost forgotten now that television has become so powerful. Television nowadays wants only the big international sports. Unless a sport can deliver a big television audience it will soon find itself out of favour.

Even athletics is struggling to find a place on television. The nation used to be glued to the box in the days of those wonderful White City meetings when the likes of Chris Chataway, Derek Ibbotson and Bill Nankeville (the father, incidentally, of comedian Bobby Davro) would battle with great athletes from all over the world. The White City was packed to the rafters and the television audience was large. Now athletics struggle to get into anyone's programme schedules. ITV, who had an exclusive contract to cover domestic athletics meetings, dumped the sport, throwing the British Athletics Federation headlong into bankruptcy. It left behind it a string of debts, many of them to athletes who hadn't been paid their agreed fees. The BBC, much to the concern of their own sports department, have agreed to take over and invest over seventeen million pounds to help the sport get back on its feet. This it is now doing under the new name of United Kingdom Athletics and led by three former international stars, David Hemery, Alan Pascoe and David Moorcroft. They have generated sponsorship worth ten million pounds over four years from an insurance company, and that income, plus the BBC money, should help restore athletics to its former glory. Much will depend on how Britain's viewing public reacts. The viewing figures will have to be good, otherwise UK Athletics could go the same way as the late unlamented British Athletics Federation.

Television has learned that sport is its big audience builder. I know what whenever a big sporting event such as the World Cup or the Olympic Games is televised people complain that there is too much sport on television, but the complainers are in the minority. Big sporting events send television's viewing figures soaring into orbit, provided the sport is of the highest quality, of course, or the viewers will give it the thumbs down.

Take, for instance, that never-to-be-forgotten Wednesday in May 1999 when Manchester United beat Bayern Munich in the final of the European Champions' League. The game between two of the titans of European football drew a British audience of 15.62 million on ITV – the nineteenth highest TV audience for a football match covered by one channel only and the fifth biggest audience for a match between two club sides.

Yet there were some things about the figures which gave us all food for thought. High though they were, they showed that only 29 per cent of the British audience watched, compared with the 37 per cent when United beat Benfica in the 1968 final. Could it be that the viewers think little of the format for the present European Champions' League when it includes teams that were not reigning champions, whereas in 1968 only the champions, the No.1 team of each country took part?

Another interesting fact is that the game did not draw the week's biggest audience; *Coronation Street* did, with 16.38 million on the Monday, and could also claim that on the Wednesday it handed over an audience of 14.6 million to the football. And just to prove that soaps are our favourite programmes, that week *Coronation Street* was Nos. 1,3 4 and 5 with *EastEnders* coming in at Nos. 6, 7 and 8 and *Emmerdale* bringing up the rear with places at No. 9, 10 and 11. The football came second.

Whatever would happen to British television if there were no football and no soaps? Even granted that you can prove anything with figures – as Disraeli once said, 'There are lies, damned lies and statistics' – the fact remains that the big audience drawers are the top sporting programmes and the soaps.

In the early years of television, sport was wary of it, and the big boys turned their backs on the new medium. They claimed that it would ruin their attendances and that television people wanted to pay peanuts for the right to cover events. There was a feeling in sport that television believed everyone with a set had a right to see the big sporting occasions. Sport believe the opposite: that television wanted to get popular programmes on the cheap.

Ignored by the big boys, television looked around for sports which did not have a wide following. They found plenty and put them on the air. All-in wrestling, for instance, lasted for many years on ITV and it turned Mick McManus into the most hated man on TV because of the roughhouse tactics he employed in the ring. I later met Mick and have played a lot of golf with him. Believe me, you could not meet a better gentleman than Mick McManus. He was obviously a great actor as well if he could make the fans think he was nothing but a roughneck dirty fighter.

Swimming was another sport delighted to get so much airtime, and would put up with all sorts of inconveniences from television producers who would keep the young swimmers (and they were all young) waiting on their starting blocks while someone would be giving the latest cricket scores, or something similar. And television did swimming a world of good, providing the opportunity for youngsters such as Anita Lonsborough, Judy Grinham and many more to become national names.

Show jumping became a big favourite on television. There were so many personality riders, people such as Pat Smythe and

David Broome, among others, who were immortalized by that magnificent commentator Dorian Williams, who sadly died far too early. I have a vivid memory of him at the 1968 Olympic Games in Mexico City where late at night we all had to work on a composite programme which was beamed to London and transmitted at breakfast time. We had to be on our toes and ready to rush into a commentary booth as soon as the previous commentator started to leave. But Dorian was never a rusher. He sat engrossed in a book. The book's title? *The Boston Strangler*. Perhaps the last book you would expect to see Dorian Williams reading.

I have mentioned those three sports because television made them popular, but now that television has time for only the major international sports, the real big time, they have more or less disappeared from the box. In the old days no one would have believed we could live without the Horse of the Year Show and the International Horse Show being given prime time. We have discovered that we can, and we do.

Meanwhile football on television has undergone a revolution. Today's equipment makes that used not all that long ago seem prehistoric. The lightweight midget cameras, the ability to put cameras and microphones in all sorts of places has turned television into an all-seeing, all-hearing entertainment medium. Inevitably, it has become too conscious of its own importance, too prone to boast of its capabilities, and there is nothing new in that. In the old days, when the spread of television was slow – painfully slow in some countries – everyone working in the industry preened themselves on each successive achievement. It was nothing to hear a continuity announcer saying something along the lines of, 'And now television takes another mammoth stride into the future. We are now going over to a passenger ship in the Atlantic Ocean to see how the passengers are enjoying themselves. So it's over to the SS *Enjoy Yourself* 1,000 miles away in mid-Atlantic.'

The enormity of prying cameras used on big, important occasions raises a more worrying question. Should television cameras be the arbiters of all that goes on during a game of football or rugby or cricket or even tiddlywinks? I say, 'No, no a thousand times no'. Television is there to bring entertainment into our homes. It is not there as the supreme being. I know television, mainly through Sky, has invested millions in football, and I know money talks. But money must never be allowed to rule our game. Already the true supporter is being denied his right to look at the fixture list and see who is playing whom and when because television now has such a big say in when games are to be played and at what time.

I met one gentleman whose firm had a box at a Premiership club, for which they had paid a lot of money. Saturday games were fine. With a three o'clock kick-off their clients were queuing up for invitations to go along for a couple of drinks or so and lunch before watching the match, and then the odd drink afterwards. But then the fixture rearrangements started. Television wanted to cover a game on a Monday night with an eight o'clock kick-off. This meant the guests arriving from their offices around six o'clock and it would be not far short of eleven o'clock at night before they left the ground. They received more 'refusals with thanks' than acceptances.

Sundays, with a four o'clock kick-off, were even more of a disaster. The invited guests were quick to point out that Sunday was the family day, with the traditional Sunday dinner. There was just no take-up for a Sunday invitation. Before long the firm discovered that their guests at many of the games were their own staff – not what the company was paying megabucks for. After just one season they decided not to renew their subscription to the box.

But for the advertisements and sponsorships I don't think Sky would be too happy with their audience, which on Sundays struggles to average one and half million viewers, and on Monday nights fails to reach the million.

There are people who cannot understand why the BBC, once the acknowledged leaders in sporting television, can no longer compete with Sky or even with ITV in sporting coverage. The main reason is money. For a licence fee of just over £100 a year you can watch all the terrestrial television stations – BBC 1 and 2, ITV, Channel Four and Channel 5. The basic satellite package plus the news and the three sports channels costs over three times that. And don't forget that you get radio thrown in for nothing with the licence fee.

Viewers, sadly, don't understand the difference between satellite and terrestrial television. Sky, the satellite station, can have three sporting channels, or more if it likes. The terrestrial companies cannot because it is impossible to get the wavelengths. So it is easy with three sporting channels to show golf all day on one, cricket all day on another and so on. But the terrestrial channels have to produce a balance of sport, drama, light entertainment and news. In other words, the whole wide spectrum of television, all on one channel, or two on the BBC.

The technical equipment now available has sent some people into cloud cuckoo land thinking that television can provide the answers to all the problems which arise on a sporting field. Cricket has solved one of its problems by having a fixed camera showing the popping crease so that if the umpire wishes to call upon the third official he can see the action and then make up his mind whether the player was run out or stumped. That and no more. Some people have campaigned for a camera at the bowler's end so that there would be fewer lbw disputes. But would there? I doubt it because lbw is always the hardest decision for an umpire to make and it is simply a matter of opinion. Would the ball have hit the wicket but for the intervention of the batsman's legs? Put three umpires at the bowler's end and you would get three different answers. Watch the replay with three of your friends and you will get *four* different verdicts.

Football fans have been loud in their calls for television replays to be used in determining the correct decision about all sorts of incidents. Sadly, Putney's ex-Member of Parliament, David Mellor, who is now chairman of the National Football Trust has jumped on the bandwagon calling for action replays to be watched by the fourth official when there is a controversial decision. Putting aside the fact that football has the widest variety of controversial decisions (look at the arguments as to whose throw-in it is), such a change would be a non-starter. Referees are human beings and make mistakes, but they are the final arbiters. The original Laws of the Game stated clearly that 'if in the opinion of the referee . . .' then the decision would be binding. Just note those words. 'If in the opinion of the referee.' Not in the opinion of either manager, either set of supporters or even the chairman of the National Football Trust.

Furthermore, football is a game of continuous action. It is not a stop-and-start game like cricket or American football, so the fans would not put up with an endless stream of stoppages while the fourth official, sitting high in the stand, was studying the replay before making his mind up whether Joe Bloggs was offside or not, or whether Joe Bloggs was tripped in the penalty area or had taken a dive. How many replays from different angles would he watch? Which angle showed the truth, the whole truth and nothing but the truth? And how would we know that the fourth official made the right interpretation from that plethora of action replays?

I was once told that someone was on the verge of perfecting a football containing a sensor capable of emitting a signal if the ball went over the line. When I asked whether this amazing piece of scientific technology would also tell us whether the man who shot or headed for goal was offside or not, my friend looked blank.

The sensor idea seems to have died a death but now we are being told that mini-cameras will be attached to the inside of goal posts and these would show clearly whether the ball had crossed the line or not. Oh, yes? And how many times would a player's body get in the way of the mini-camera so that all the fourth official would see is the backside of a footballer? And would those cameras be moveable so that we could see if the ball had crossed the line mid-air?

Let us get on with the game as it was meant to be played and refereed and let us be thankful to television for bringing the action into the homes of those who can't make it to the matches. Let us have television as entertainment, not as judge and jury. Because the camera does lie, you know. Often.

One change in television coverage of football over the years has not been for the better: the downgrading of the commentator. More often than not the commentator gets no credit in the newspaper or even from the actual television station. It is all 'Presented by . . .' The presenter has what we in Lancashire call 'a bobby's job'. He waffles on in the studio with two pundits and only at the last minute calls on the commentator, who is the man who has done his homework and has worked out how he is going to tackle the real job, the difficult job of doing the commentary.

Without the commentator the presenters would be helpless.

A commentator's job is to add to the picture, to identify the players and to remind the viewers of the score and the time, because those tiny captions in the screen's top left-hand corner are invisible to all but those with magnificent eyesight. I read an interview with a commentator once who said he was a football fan. (So are all commentators otherwise they would never have taken the job.) He went on to add that he commentates like a fan. All I can say is that is the one thing he should never do. Directors are largely to blame for insisting that commentators should make the game exciting. Not all games are exciting, so it is no use trying to kid the public. They can see what is going on.

The commentators seem scared to death of remaining silent even for the shortest time. How often have you heard one say something like, 'And now it's Giggs . . . It's still Giggs . . . It's *still* Giggs . . . oh! He's shot wide.' Once we have had Giggs identified we don't need to be reminded that he still has the ball. We can see that.

Few of the summarizers add anything to the game. For instance, we see a run down the wing, the ball is centred and one of the strikers leaps into the air and heads over the bar. That is usually translated by the summarizer as 'That was a great run down the wing and a beautifully flighted centre to the far post. The striker was unlucky that his header went over the bar.' All of which we could clearly see. The best summarizer I have heard is David Pleat. Here is a man who knows his football and knows his television as well. He doesn't describe what the viewers have seen but in a few words gives a clear analysis of what has just happened.

Another pitfall for a commentator is including useless information or giving useful information at the wrong time.

When a player is bearing down on goal and is likely to score it is not really the time to remind us that his hobbies are growing tomatoes and playing badminton, and it is hardly likely to be of much interest to remind us that in a game last season he scored a hat-trick and then missed a penalty.

There is a wonderful story about Henry Longhurst, the greatest of all golf commentators. He was always stationed at the last par 3 hole for the Augusta Masters and once he told us, 'And on the tee is Arnold Palmer of the United States, who is three under par today and eleven under par for the tournament. It looks as if he's taking a six iron.'

The ball landed safely on the green, leaving Palmer with a very good chance of a birdie two. Well, what else would you expect of Arnold Palmer? Longhurst reckoned that was just the sort of shot Palmer would play so he made no comment.

The American director, unaccustomed to commentators being silent, let out a howl of 'What's happened to that goddam limey? Has he died?'

No, Henry was still alive and behaving as a good commentator should.

In the memorable 1970 Open Championship at St Andrews when Doug Saunders of the United States missed the putt on the 18th green of the final round and so had to play off with Jack Nicklaus, Henry did it again. As Saunders looked carefully at the line of his putt, Henry announced that 'Doug Saunders needs this putt for the Championship.' Saunders then bent forward to brush away an imaginary piece of grass, a sure sign that he was having an attack of the yipps. Longhurst's only comment was an ominous, 'Oh, dear.'

Eventually Saunders putted and the ball went straight for the hole but at the last split second turned off to the right. Modern commentary would demand screams of 'He's missed it! Doug

Saunders has blown his chance of an Open victory. That putt could cost him millions of dollars,' and so forth.

The majestic Henry Longhurst uttered not a single word. It was the best piece of television sporting commentary I have ever heard. After all, he had set the scene, told us Saunders needed the putt to win. The 'Oh, dear' suggested the yipps. So when the ball missed the hole we could all see that . . . well, he had missed.

Prospective commentators should remember that incident and learn from it. To be good at the job you must not be biased, you must identify and if you cannot add to the picture you must keep your mouth shut. You certainly don't need to scream.

But my greatest gripe about the coverage of just about all sports these days by television, radio and the newspapers is the passion for statistics, or that awful abbreviation stats. I yawn my head off when I see captions telling us how many attempts on goal each side has made and how many were on target, how many corners each side has had and all sorts of other meaningless statistics. There is only one statistic that matters as far as a football match is concerned and that is how many goals each side scored.

Many years ago I commentated on a match at Filbert Street, Leicester, between Leicester City and Manchester United. You can get some idea how long ago it was from the fact that the Leicester City manager was a Scot by the name of Matt Gillies and the Manchester United manager was another Scot and another Matt – Matt Busby.

The game has been shown on the *Bobby Charlton Scrapbook* on Sky – in fact it has been shown more than once. Leicester forced forty-four corners in the match, whereas Manchester United didn't get a single one. The counting, incidentally, was not done by me but by some statistician and the figures were confirmed by Matt Gillies in the post-match interview. Leicester City 44 corners – Manchester United 0. Could you get a better statistic to demonstrate Leicester's supremacy? However, Manchester United scored five goals and Leicester City didn't score at all. Leicester City, forty-four corners and no goals; Manchester United, no corners and five goals. Which would you prefer?

And, incidentally, apologies to my good friend Gordon Banks for including this story in the book. Gordon was the Leicester City goalkeeper that day!

Much more recently, George Graham, manager of Arsenal at the time, made the same point brilliantly in an interview for *Match of the Day* after a game against Sheffield Wednesday which Arsenal had just won 2–1. The interviewer ended by saying, 'George, I felt sorry for Wednesday. They played very well and frankly I thought they deserved at least one point. So why do you think they lost?'

George Graham flashed that disarming smile of his and replied, 'Simply because we scored twice and they only scored once.' As they say after solving a geometry problem, QED.

19

My Game Heading
the Wrong Way

Football. I have loved it all my lifc. I wish I had thought of calling it 'The Beautiful Game' before the great Pelé did, because it is the beautiful game if it is played properly. But now I worry about my old friend. I have a feeling that it has taken the wrong road, that it is wandering into a whole heap of trouble. Nonsense, you might say, the game is as popular as ever, if not more so. That may be true, but it certainly hasn't got the feeling it once had.

Sky Television, realizing football's great popularity, has pumped millions of pounds into it, and fans should be thankful for it. But there is a snag. The money has not been used either fairly or wisely. In the football world now the rich get richer and the poor get poorer.

Once upon a time when the Football League consisted of four divisions with an excellent system of promotion and relegation, we had the strongest league system in the world. Today we don't, because the rich clubs want to grab all they can get – and it is easy for them to get it – and they have little or no thought for those less fortunate.

The breakaway of the Premiership from the Football League was the first step in the wrong direction. Already the big clubs had won the rights to keep their gate receipts and there was some justification for that. After all, it was hardly fair for Manchester United, with attendances topping 50,000 for each home game, having to share that gate with a club, say, like Southampton which can only offer the share of a 15,000 gate in return. But the first sign of greed arose when the Premiership was supposed to reduce itself to eighteen clubs.

The clubs realized that they would lose two lucrative home games so they decided to stick to a twenty-club formation, thus incurring the wrath of UEFA. And it soon became obvious that the Premiership, having torn itself away from the Football League, was intent on having a two-tier Premiership. The television money was not divided equally, the rich clubs began to coin money, the less fashionable clubs began to struggle.

So the Premiership has become a league of five clubs – Manchester United, Arsenal, Leeds United, Liverpool and Chelsea. One of those five would win the title, three of the remaining fifteen would be relegated. They would be replaced by three clubs from the First Division, who would not have the financial clout to hold their own. The odds were always on the three promoted clubs to be relegated after just one season with the big boys, and this would put them into financial trouble because in the Premiership they would have to pay Premiership wages and the players would not accept reductions if they were relegated.

If the bottom section of the Premiership is a large danger area, the top echelon is composed of just a few élite clubs. In the seven seasons of the Premiership so far, only three clubs have won the title: Arsenal and Blackburn Rovers have each won it once; Manchester United have won in the other five seasons.

With so much money going into their coffers from television, the élite of the Premiership have been able to pay huge transfer fees and enormous wages to lure foreign stars to our game. Some of the foreign players have been excellent buys but many have been money misspent. Many people believe that with so much money at the top the gravy-train must spread to all four divisions. But it doesn't. Yet even Third Division players have agents who often hold the clubs to ransom, so making their financial plight worse.

Players' agents, according to many in the game, are guilty of making ever-spiralling wage demands and transfer fees. That is not exactly true. There are some agents I would not like to deal with, but that applies to all other professions, not just football, and it would be wrong to suggest all agents are bad. Some look after their players well and fairly, and it is only right that players, who are not well versed in legal and financial matters, should have someone to represent them when it comes to discussions about terms of contracts.

The dreadful thing about football is that contracts are not worth the paper on which they are written, and it has always been so. Managers and players have suffered alike. Johnny Carey was sacked from his job as Everton's manager in a taxicab on the way to Euston station after a Football League meeting, when Everton at the time were third in the old First Division. Another manager was given a vote of confidence by his chairman on Saturday, invited to the chairman's house for Sunday lunch and sacked on Monday.

Today's transfer market and huge wage scales have risen to an obscene level. Lazio, who just failed to win the Italian championship in the 1998–99 season, have sold Christian Vieri, their international striker, to Inter Milan for a staggering £32 million. There is no doubt that Vieri is a fine player, but £32 million? Come off it! He has only been in Serie A since 1995 when he moved to Atlanta from the Second division. In 1996 he moved to Juventus for just over two million and scored fourteen goals in thirty-seven games. The following year he changed the scenery to Spain, to Atletico Madrid to be exact. They paid £12 million for him, which wasn't a bad piece of business by Juventus. He played twenty-four Spanish league games and averaged a goal a game, then at the end of the season he packed his bags again and was off to Lazio for £17 million. So, in just one season, Lazio have doubled their money and Vieri is banking an annual salary of a mere four million pounds. I wonder where he will go in the year 2000? To another rich Italian club? Maybe, but remember there is something of the gypsy in Vieri. He is a have-boots-will-travel sort of guy.

Maybe, then, he will decide to go and help Australia qualify for the 2006 World Cup. No, don't laugh because Christian Vieri was brought up in Australia. His parents emigrated there in 1978. Believe it or not, Christian is a fair cricketer and really loves the game. Perhaps if he went back to Australia he might even make the Aussies' Test team. He is young enough (only twenty-five) but the transfer fee might be beyond the Australian Cricket Board.

To make up for the loss of Vieri, Lazio tried to sign Nicholas Anelka from Arsenal. The fee mentioned was a ridiculous £22 million, which led Michael Parkinson to write in his *Daily Telegraph* column, 'If Anelka is worth £22 million I am a pork chop.' Well, Michael is no pork chop. A Barnsley chop maybe, but not a pork chop.

Lazio could afford such a ridiculous fee after their transfer of Vieri for crazy money, and Arsenal, who had signed Anelka two years previously for a mere half a million and seen him have just one season in the Premiership, were more than happy to complete the deal and make a massive profit. It all goes to show the millions that can be made by buying and selling players.

But the Anelka saga unearthed another shady side of the game's wheeling and dealing. Arsenal wanted to keep the player but Anelka had set his heart on joining Real Madrid. In fact he, or his two brothers who act as his agent, had, it seemed, told Real Madrid that he would be joining them. Then the news was broken to Arsenal.

Now Arsenal don't do business like that. They pointed out to Anelka that he was still under contract to them and he wasn't free to leave without their agreement. That peeved Anelka and his two brothers, who didn't seem to set any store by the contract.

Arsenal were now in a dilemma. A player they had under contract and whom they didn't want to transfer insisted that he was going to leave and play for Real Madrid. Arsenal could have told the player that there was no way he was leaving and let him stew in the reserve side until the end of his contract.

By the time his contract was up he would be a forgotten player worth nothing on the transfer market. On the other hand Arsenal would have to pay his agreed wages as stipulated in the contract, and these were considerable. They also faced losing a large capital gain. Far better then to sell the player to anyone who matched their asking price of more than £20 million, and agreed to Anelka's personal terms, which were reported to be well over £50,000 as week, or, as the Italians put it, over 70 billion lire. But the player insisted on joining Real Madrid

The negotiations for the 20-year-old with limited experience and an inflated idea of his own talents went on and on and became more and more curious until quite frankly most people were fed up to the back teeth with the name of Nicholas Anelka. But was he to blame, or was it his two brothers-cum-agents who were the trouble makers? Or was it the system itself? Who knows? But one thing is certain . . . the transfer market has become ridiculous . . . and dangerous.

How long this madness can go on nobody knows, but the fact remains that while there are over 200 foreign footballers in the Premiership alone, there were 700 home-grown players made surplus to requirements at the end of June 1999, the date on which contracts expired.

Why do the big clubs go shopping abroad? Simply because they can buy a cheaper player with top-class experience on the continent for half the price they are asked for a home-grown player who has never sampled Premiership football. What would you do, go for a footballer of experience who would cost three million pounds or risk six or seven million on a player who has sampled nothing higher than the First Division and may not make a higher grade successfully?

Everything these days depends on money but banks are not as generous as they used to be with loans. That is why more and more clubs find administrators or liquidators arriving on their premises. The average fan cannot comprehend the tightrope which so many clubs are walking. If a few results go against them they write to the newspapers demanding that the directors put their hands in their pockets and buy such-and-such a player. Little do they realize how much directors have ploughed into the club and there must be a limit to anyone's budget. Nor do the fans realize how parlous is the state of the club finances. Those clubs which have become public limited companies are a little more fortunate because they can invest in outside activities such as hotels, leisure centres, conference centres and other such money-makers. But public limited companies have to answer to their shareholders before they answer to the fans.

The ruling bodies, like FIFA, which controls world football, and UEFA, which rules European football, don't help. They are too keen on organizing ever more international competitions, which clutter up fixture lists and make money for FIFA and UEFA but nothing for the clubs not in the big competitions. At one time there were three important tournaments – the World Cup and the European Championships, both for national teams, and the European Cup for the champion club in each European country. Things have changed. The World Cup is still with us every four years, with nations vying with each other for the honour of staging the finals. Likewise the European Championships. Not so the European Cup. Now it is called the European Champions' League and UEFA has allowed ever more teams into a competition which was originally for champions only. England, for instance, have three sides in the current competition.

It is a devious way of trying to get a European Superleague in by the back door. If it succeeds it will devalue national football throughout the continent, and rob loyal fans of the right to enjoy and support home games. Football as we have loved it will eventually die, except for the very rich clubs which will flit across Europe playing each other in a competition which will rob millions of true football fans of their pleasure.

Just pause for a moment and think of where football will be played in Britain if the Superleague planners win. Arsenal, Manchester United and Newcastle United will be England's representatives because they are rich clubs with splendid stadiums. (Arsenal will have to move from Highbury, where the capacity is too low and car parking space non-existent, so they will probably buy Chelsea Village) and geographically these clubs cover the North, the Midlands and the South. Scotland will have Celtic and Rangers, although knowing how the minds of the planners work they will probably ask the two clubs to merge.

And what happens to the rest of the Premiership and the Football League? Who cares? If you cannot get to Arsenal, Manchester United and Newcastle United then *tough*. Anyway, even if you do, you will have to pay megabucks to get in because, remember, this is no longer about football. This is about money. And after all, you can join in the fun for something like £10 a throw (at the start) and watch it on Pay Television.

That is why I am worried about the beautiful game I love, the beautiful game which has brought so much pleasure to so many people. It is the beautiful game which is being slowly put to death.

Please, somebody, come and save my old friend.

20

Extra Time

My publishers have decided that I should not be allowed to rest after writing this book. They reckon I should be made to play a bit of extra time, which means telling a few tales which have nothing to do with anything, but you might find them amusing. So to the kick-off for the first half of extra time.

Alec and Eric Bedser are inseparable. They are not just twins, they are real lookalikes. Just after the war Alec was selected to go on the MCC tour to Australia. Eric wasn't. But a London evening newspaper decided to send him, anyway, to report the tour. They booked him in steerage as opposed to the team's more luxurious first-class accommodation. But since no one can tell Alec and Eric apart, Eric spent more time in first class than he did down below.

When they landed in Australia, Alec went off to have a haircut. On his return to the hotel Eric was there and Alec gave him directions to the barber's shop. Within ten minutes of Alec leaving it, Eric entered the shop. The barber took one look and said, 'Cor, your bloody hair grows quickly, cobber.'

Everybody knows that Sir Geoff Hurst is the only man to have scored a hat-trick in a World Cup Final. But how many remember that at Wembley in 1966 he scored England's first goal with his *head*, the third goal (his second) with his *right* foot and the fourth goal (the 'it's all over' goal) with his *left* foot. It's a good job England didn't call on him to score another!

One radio programme I have always admired is *Radio Five Live*, and I was happy to present two nostalgic programmes for them. One was on people's memories of 1966 World Cup Final day. We gathered loads of material, including an interview with one of the handful of people who went on to the pitch thinking it was all over . . just before it was. The programme needed some brilliant editing so I was thankful that the producer was Audrey Adams, who did such a great job that I will forgive her for being a Watford supporter and also for being so delighted that Watford beat Bolton Wanderers in last season's play-off for a place in the Premiership.

The other programme was also about 1966. It was one of a short series highlighting the greatest sporting years of the past. Now 1966 was the year of the World Cup win but it was also the year of Arkle, the great steeplechaser, and I went to interview the wonderful Duchess of Westminster, who owned and loved Arkle.

Two of her answers will stick with me for ever. I explained that the format of the programmes was to highlight the sporting events of 1966 and that we could not leave out Arkle. She replied, 'I should think not. After all, what else happened in the sporting world in 1966?'

I then asked her why, if Arkle was such a great steeplechaser, she had never entered him for the Grand National. Her answer was, 'Do you think I would let a classic horse like Arkle mix with a lot of hooligan horses at Aintree?'

*

Lena, our daughter, always telephoned home on a Sunday (cheap rate calls, you see) and she kept this up after my wife died. One Sunday I was on my way to Paris for a television show and realized Lena would be telephoning and getting only the answerphone, so I rang her from Heathrow. She asked me what I was doing there and I told her I was flying to Paris to record a television show. The conversation went like this:

LENA: 'What's the show about?'
ME: 'I don't know anything about it. It's something called *Eurotrash*.
LENA (*after a long pause*: 'Dad, you can't go on that. It's obscene.'

But I went to Paris and appeared on the show as the commentator when Lolo Ferrari played blow football against Martin Peters and then Ramon Vega.

When Lena told her two daughters, Sarah and Amy, what I was going to do they smiled knowingly. Her son, David, a pupil at Torquay Grammar School, told all the lads at school and they were not just envious, they thought I was privileged, especially in so far as I was meeting Lolo Ferrari.

San Francisco is a wonderful city and I can understand why that fellow left his heart there. Once when I was there I was told how to ride the trolleys, which went 'Clang, Clang' for Judy Garland and go right up to Fisherman's Wharf. The trolleys are always crowded so when the ticket collector comes round you tell him that Charlie has your ticket and you point to someone hemmed in by the crowd. Or if you are foreign, just talk in your mother-tongue. Americans can't be bothered with people who speak strange languages. Even if your mother-tongue is English just jabber away and the ticket collector will assume you are a dim-witted foreigner and you will get away with it. But don't think you can get away with it again on the return journey. You have to queue at Fisherman's Wharf and buy your ticket before you get on the trolley for the trip back to downtown San Francisco.

Jan Sewell, who has helped so much in the editing of this book, is a very good friend of mine, but she does get me into all sorts of scrapes. We went on a tour of San Francisco together and at one stop we both fancied a non-alcoholic drink. We found a bar with a huge man sitting on a bar stool, reading a magazine. The bar owner came in and said he was just getting some beer in, so our huge friend offered to serve us. I ordered two Bloody Mary mixes, which are small bottles of the spiced tomato juice and sometimes called Virgin Marys. I was looking at some of the notices on the wall and when I turned round and saw the stand-in barman had taken two pint glasses and half filled them with vodka. He then added the tomato juice, Tabasco, Worcestershire sauce, horseradish, lime, salt, pepper, celery and probably a dash of engine oil. It all added up to the finest Bloody Mary I have ever tasted, despite the fact that all we both wanted was the Bloody Mary mix. The cost for the two drinks was just six dollars.

The owner told us that they didn't have much mid-day trade. They were very busy in the evening but he didn't think it was the sort of place we would like to visit. Our suspicions were confirmed and we agreed with him. But with two pints of Bloody Mary for just six dollars, well . . .

The late Godfrey Evans was not only one of the greatest wicket-keepers who ever crouched behind the stumps, but he was also one of sport's greatest characters. Once when we were playing in the same charity golf day he came over to me as I was having dinner. He had a bottle of wine about one-third full or two-thirds empty, depending on whether you are an optimist or a pessimist, and as he refilled his glass from my bottle he said that he never worried about how much of the tab the sponsors were picking up. 'I just sign for everything,' he said, 'and you find out when you are leaving how much the sponsor is paying and how much you are expected to contribute. If you pay cash you might fork out for something the sponsors would have picked up.'

Good thinker was our Godfrey!

One of the great joys of the overseas trips was that it was a million to one that Geoffrey Green, The Association Football correspondent of *The Times*, as his newspaper called him, would be on the trip. Geoffrey was a brilliant writer, a man of great bohemian charm to whom everyone was 'my old commander' and every day was Christmas Day.

On one trip to Brazil, we of the media were invited to a monumental party in Sao Paulo, and as night was turning into dawn I was talking to some Brazilians who wanted to know my views on the colour bar. (You have to remember that Brazilians are jet black or Persil white and every colour in between those two extremes.) Geoffrey suddenly appeared and one of my companions asked him if he believed in the colour bar.

Geoffrey replied, 'No, I believe in the colours of the rainbow.'

The Brazilians were delighted and asked Geoffrey and me to join them for dawn now that the night had all but disappeared, so the pair of us, along with five Brazilians, got into a car which was driven as only a Brazilian can drive a car – at breakneck and with little or no regard for anyone else on the road.

I began to suspect that we were being kidnapped, but we were in no such danger. We were just the victims of typical Brazilian hospitality and we were soon in a wayside cafe high in the mountains. The furniture was very basic but one of our friends began to drum his fingertips on the top of the wooden table. Another just tapped on the top of a matchbox, while a third pushed and pulled a single match in and out of an empty matchbox.

This produced the sound of a string instrument while the fourth member of the party just rubbed two paper napkins together which gave the sound of the samba. Friend number five began to sing to this strange musical accompaniment.

The dawn broke into daylight and both Geoffrey and I were hypnotised by the simple music and the lovely singing, the like of which we had never heard before. I spent many dawns in Geoffrey Green's company, but none surpassed this one.

I was once told you have not lived until you have seen the Rome derby between Roma and Lazio, so one Saturday I made sure I was there at Rome's famous Stadio Olimpico. Roma and Lazio share the ground, but this was designated as Roma's home game. The atmosphere beat anything I had ever experienced at an English derby. When the Roma team appeared banners suddenly shot down from the roof of the stand to ground level, and the fans held up cards coloured alternately red and yellow, the Roma colours. It was an amazing spectacle.

After the match a car took me back to my hotel, where I had a drink in the bar and charged it to my room, then went up to shave and shower. I emptied my pockets and discovered to my horror that I had only a 1,000 lire note, which wouldn't buy you anything. My pocket had been brilliantly picked and £140-worth of Italian currency was now owned by someone else. I was told to claim off my insurance but to make a valid claim you have to go to the police and if you went to a Rome police station and said, 'I wish to report that my pocket has been picked,' you would be told, 'Join the end of the queue. It's only twenty kilometres long.'

The day after that Rome derby, which was played on a Saturday, it was difficult to change money. I got some from the hotel at a dreadful rate, but Jan and I sat at a pavement café on the Via Veneto having vodka and tonics and watching the world go by. When the bill came I hadn't got enough money and the bar would not accept credit cards. So I had to walk a good quarter of a mile to my hotel to get some more lire and meanwhile, as the waitress said, 'signora' had to wait where she was. As a hostage. After I had changed some money a thought about not going back to the bar did cross my mind, but then . . . no, I'm too nice a fellow to do a thing like that to a lovely lady.

On another occasion, Jan and I were having dinner on the Via Veneto and Jan spotted a couple having their wine served out of a jug. So the following night, Jan, who speaks as much Italian as I speak Greek, tried to get through to the wine waiter that we would like some strong rustic wine. He turned up with a bottle of their most expensive wine and I said, 'We'll have that.' He poured it and it was magnificent. When our first course came I reached for the olive oil, the sleeve of my light-blue silk jacket touched the bottle of excruciatingly expensive and beautiful wine and it poured all over my expensive and lovely silk jacket which was ruined. Jan has promised not to order strong, rustic wine in an Italian restaurant again.

End of extra time and no penalty shoot-out necessary.